Original 2001 watercolor of "Classic" Forestry Building. *Courtesy Jill Leite, Jill*

The Georgia Forestry Association and the Warnell School of Forestry and Natural Resources at the University of Georgia are proud to sponsor *The Centennial History of Forestry in Georgia: A Pictorial Journey,* which honors the legacy of forestry in the great state of Georgia.

The
Centennial History
of Forestry in Georgia

A Pictorial Journey

By
Bob Izlar
2006
D0827

Contributors
Morgan Nolan
Bonnell H. Stone
Leon S. Brown
&
Warnell School of Forestry and Natural Resources

Foreword
Chuck Leavell

Dedication

To the men and women of Georgia's forestry community who gave their lives in service to their country.

Cover photo courtesy *photospin.com*, 2000

The Donning Company Publishers
184 Business Park Drive, Suite 206
Virginia Beach, VA 23462-6533

Steve Mull, General Manager
Barbara Buchanan, Office Manager
Kathleen Sheridan, Senior Editor
Lynn Parrott, Graphic Designer
Amy Thomann, Imaging Artist
Scott Rule, Director of Marketing and Cover Design
Stephanie Linneman, Marketing Coordinator
Lori Kennedy, Project Research Coordinator

B. L. Walton Jr., Project Director

Library of Congress Cataloging-in-Publication Data
Izlar, Robert Lee, 1949-
  The centennial history of forestry in Georgia : a pictorial journey / by Bob Izlar ; contributors: Morgan Nolan, Bonnell H. Stone, Leon S. Brown ; foreword Chuck Leavell.
      p. cm.
  Includes bibliographical references and index.
  ISBN-13: 978-1-57864-348-6 (hard cover : alk. paper)
  ISBN-10: 1-57864-348-1
  1. Forests and forestry—Georgia—History. 2. Forests and forestry—Georgia—Pictorial works. I. Title.
  SD144.G4I95 2006
  634.909758'022—dc22

                                    2005035258

Printed in the United States of America by Walsworth Publishing Company

Courtesy C. Evan, UGA, forestryimages.org

Contents

Foreword

The forest is a place where we struggle endlessly for balance.[1]

My love of our family forest Charlane, our state's and nation's forests, and the trees is as hard to express as my love for my family or for a good song. These things are so deep, I couldn't breathe if they weren't part of my life.[2] I've been very fortunate to have had a wonderful career in music, playing with some of the greatest artists of our time, including the Rolling Stones, Eric Clapton, the Allman Brothers Band, George Harrison, and others. The rush from getting some hot licks in is incredible, but I also treasure the peace I get riding a tractor on my tree farm.

To me, life is all about balance. A musical group and musical instruments must all play in concert; they must have that proper balance that produces that perfect sound. I try to have balance in my life between my music career, my family, and my forest. In forestry, all the players involved must play the same tune, just like in music. We have to work together, just like a band. It takes everybody from foresters to environmentalists, from private landowners to everyday citizens, from the media to politicians and policy makers, from loggers and truckers to wood consuming mills, and from teachers to investors to make the great forestry song sound right.

The Rolling Stones is composed of four very talented individuals—Mick Jagger, Keith Richards, Charlie Watts, and Ronnie Wood. They each have a special style and talent they bring to the band. Each of them has produced very successful solo albums but nothing like Team Rolling Stones. They understand that and the value of teamwork and that the whole is greater than the sum of its parts.

This book is the story of a great team—the Warnell School of Forestry and Natural Resources and the Georgia Forestry Association. I consider it a personal honor to claim close affiliation to both groups. I'm very proud to say I'm an adopted Bulldog because of my status as Honorary Alumnus of the School of Forest Resources. My lovely wife, Rose Lane, and I are very proud also of the scholarship fund established at the School in our names. My work for the Georgia Forestry Association in the Georgia We Grow Trees public relations campaign, Tree Farm, and Project Learning Tree has been enlightening and rewarding. The friendships and experiences will be with me a long time. May Georgia's beautiful forests thrive forever!

Chuck Leavell
1999 National Tree Farmer of the Year
Rolling Stones keyboardist and musical director
November 4, 2005

Preface

The Forest History Society says, "The Forest is a vessel of time. Beneath its canopy echo vital stories from our past, revealing an elaborate history to those who will listen. The human narrative is forever one of progress and difficult decisions, and nowhere does the story unfold more dramatically than in the heart of the forest." The heart of Georgia is its people for sure; however, for our entire history, the forest has been inextricably linked to our people. Time and time again, Georgians have used the forest as a lever to pull themselves out of hard times, and we have certainly seen our share of hard times from drought, fire, boll weevils, hurricanes, pine beetles, economic depression, the "cut out and get out" logging era, and the utter horror of war "up close and personal."

The story of Georgia forestry is a story of people in love with the land, a people with a Faulknerian sense of place, a people with a sense of duty to the land and future generations, and two great organizations that sprang from the people. In this book, I attempt to tell the story of the influence of these two groups on Georgia and Georgians over the past century.

A few noble Georgians had the extreme long-range vision and wisdom to sense a need for a School of Forestry and Natural Resources where natural resource professionals could be trained to take their rightful place in restoring and conserving our precious natural resources. Some of those same Georgians sensed the urgency to have an organization that would work in concert with the School of Forestry and Natural Resources and become an advocate for the forest and future generations. So, just one year after the founding of the school in the hills of north Georgia, the Georgia Forestry Association was established in Athens. The legacy these two groups have combined to create is remarkable, and it is a legacy the citizens of Georgia can be thankful for.

So, this is the story of a journey over a hundred years taken by a people, individuals, a state, corporations, and two organizations with a dream they could make things better. It is a journey of hope and renewal. Once again, the Forest History Society eloquently states the value of remembering this journey through time:

> *To the forest we come for magnificence and bounty—to make more of ourselves than we can ever be without it. Whether we are asking for resources or refuge, the forest is where we struggle endlessly for balance. What will we give and what will we take? When we answer these questions well we are made better, when we are wrong we hope to learn from our misjudgment... If we pay close attention and value what we learn, we will enjoy a deeper connection to the forest today and a more advantageous position to encounter it tomorrow.*

I read once in an old *Pandora* something along the lines of, "The task of disarming criticism is a fruitless one." More than likely, this book will be criticized for any number of reasons and probably most of them justified. But let me say what this book is not. It is not a history of Georgia forestry and certainly not the definitive history. That was done by Dr. I. James Pikl, Jr., in his excellent *A History of Georgia Forestry*, which covered things from 1540 to 1965. The Georgia Forestry Association underwrote that publication and furnished much of the background material. There is no way I could possibly cover the long sweep of history as he did, nor as well. The curious incident of the German shepherd, the Shetland pony episode and the prurient interest in the 1972 *Cypress Knee* are best left to other writers and other times.

I was asked by WSFNR Dean Dick Porterfield and GFA Executive Vice President Steve McWilliams to write the centennial history of the University of Georgia School of Forestry and Natural Resources and Georgia Forestry Association. In so doing, I have tried to faithfully review the major milestones and events in roughly that one hundred-year time frame. Maybe by coincidence I have hit on covering "the history of Georgia forestry" in the very arduous task of trying to describe the contributions of both organizations to the state, nation and world through forestry. Don't expect this to be in the same gilt-edged class as Dr. James E. Fickle's companion volumes *Timber: A Photographic History of Mississippi Forestry* and *Mississippi Forests and Forestry*. I'm not a historian by training, only a forester who has always loved history. Nor am I a "pedantic gerund grinding" writer, as a cursory glance at my high school or university transcripts will reveal. Any proper use of the Queen's English here is not by design but through the thoughtful patience and corrections of others.

Yet, I've been told repeatedly by my "friends" that I'm the perfect person to write this because I'm the only one who has been around long enough to have actually graduated from one of the book's sponsoring organizations and worked for both. Hardly a sterling qualification. Some have even alluded to the fact that I personally knew George Foster Peabody, Chancellors Hill and Barrow, Dean Akerman, and Secretary Bonnell Stone. I know I probably look that old, but I usually appear that way because on some days I feel the Deity created the entire universe for my personal inconvenience.

In researching this book, I was given a letter by Dr. Klaus Steinbeck, my old Forest Ecology and Silviculture Professor and dear friend. It is a letter from Dr. Jack T. May, Professor Emeritus, to then Dean Arnett Mace. Jack wrote two pages of advice on how a book such as this present one should be written (leaving out the GFA history, I might add). He ended the letter with, "It will be a challenge to get this story written and published by 2006." Some challenge it was, Jack!

Nevertheless, this project has been a tremendously rewarding one for me. Despite being "that" old, I actually learned a lot about the history of the School, the Association and State that I guess I must have forgotten in the last hundred years. For me, forestry has been an education, a profession, a calling, a cause and a life. So, my feeble attempt at bringing to the fore the best Georgia forestry has had to offer over the last century has been a personal honor. I'm sure others could have done an infinitely better job, but they are not old enough.

Guide Tree Farm
Veterans Day, 2005

Acknowledgments

At a small cost are men educated to make leather into shoes; but at a great cost, what am I educated to make?—Sir Thomas Carlyle[1]

I've learned many valuable lessons in my military service, from my cadet days in 1967 to the present. One of those is the saying (which Joe Hopkins, my old South Georgia hunting buddy, takes delight in), "Never miss the meal in front of you because you never know when you'll eat again" as well as "If the enemy is in range, so are you" and "Officers eat last." But the best thing I learned and try to remember every day is a well-known Army dictum: "You never accomplish anything unless somebody helps you." Well, I have received much help on this book, and to all who gave help I sincerely thank you and remain in your debt.

I've had very few original ideas for this book. While the name of the special profile series— "Champions of Forestry"—is my idea, the idea to single out special but representative forestry leaders was Dr. James Pikl's in his landmark book. I merely copied him, although the choice of those profiled was mine. However, I'd like to express my gratitude to the following for providing background information, key dates, important biographical details, and a review of the drafts: Andy Stone and Greg Griffith, Stuckey Timberland; Donna Perry and Marshall Thomas, F & W Forestry Services; Barbara Weitzer and Carol McKernan, Society of American Foresters; Sharon Smith and Larry Thompson, T & S Hardwoods, Inc.; Bonner Jones; Mamie Woodlief, Herty Foundation; Joe Hopkins, Toledo Manufacturing Company; Charley Tarver, Forest Investment Associates; J. Reid Parker; Fred Haeussler; Bill Oettmeier, Jr., Superior Pine Products Company; Chuck Leavell, Charlane Plantation; Donnie Warren and Harley Langdale, Jr., the Langdale Company; Alex W. Patterson, Alston and Bird; Fran Lancaster; Claude Yearwood, the Price Company; Hugh Gillis, Sr., Gillis Ag and Timber, Inc.; Jim L. Gillis, Jr., Soperton Naval Stores, Inc.; and Mike Clutter, Hargreaves Distinguished Professor of Forest Finance, UGA Center for Forest Business.

For the wonderful photos in this book I'm grateful to Steve McWilliams, Dick Porterfield, and Helen Fosgate for putting out the call for help in gathering pictures. The following people and organizations graciously responded and provided permission to print: John Poole, Georgia Pulp and Paper Association; Dr. Jacek P. Siry, UGA Center for Forest Business and Herty Foundation Board; Steve Crawford, Jr., Steve Crawford Forest Products, Inc.; Alva Hopkins and Carla Rapp, GFA; Lee Rhodes, Rhodes Timber; the late Moneta Hewitt, Hebard Lumber Company; Donna Perry, F & W Forestry Services; Mike Bell and Sid Gray, Rayonier; Jerry Lanser, Bev Griffin, and Janet McRanie, Weyerhaeuser Company; Deborah Baker, Charley Hood, and Robert A. Burns, Georgia-Pacific Corporation; Jenny Yearwood, Amanda Newman, J. P. Bond, and Sara Johnson, WSFNR; Rachel

Crumbley and Rob Kindrick, Callaway Gardens; Kirsten Smith, Plum Creek Timber Company; Tom Trembath and Charley Tarver, Forest Investment Associates; Frank Montfort Riley, Jr., Scofield Timber; Sam Killian; Geoff Hill and Jim Rakestraw, International Paper Company; Harley Langdale, Jr., Andres Villegas, and Jim Hickman, the Langdale Company; Bill Barton; Fred Haeussler; Dr. Mike Clutter, UGA Center for Forest Business; Bill Oettmeier, Jr., Superior Pine Products Company; Brian Stone, Forest Resource Consultants; Chuck and Rose Lane Leavell, Charlane Plantation; Bob Lazenby; Ken Stewart and Sharon Dolliver, Georgia Forestry Commission; Rob Sumner; Joe Hopkins, Toledo Manufacturing Company; Jim L. Gillis, Jr., and Hugh Gillis, Sr.; Larry Thompson, T & S Hardwoods, Inc.; University of Georgia Warnell School of Forestry and Natural Resources; Fran Lancaster; Dr. Harry Wiant; Walter Jarck; Pamela Petersen-Frey, A4, Inc.; James P. "Buster" Herrin; Andy Stone, Stuckey Timberland, Inc.; Bonner Jones; George D. "Ted" Walker; Steven A. Brown, University of Georgia Library; Jill Leite, Jill Leite Studio; Sarah Strum, Forest Landowners Association; and Randy Aglin.

Special thanks to these individuals and organizations for permission to use their logos: Dick Porterfield, Warnell School of Forestry and Natural Resources; Steve McWilliams and Carla Rapp, GFA; Dr. Cecil Jennings, Unit Leader, Georgia Cooperative Fish & Wildlife Unit; Steve Castleberry of WSFNR and Jane Pelkey of the Wildlife Society; Billy Humphries of Forest Resource Consultants and Sarah O'Neil of the Association of Consulting Foresters; Dr. Aaron Fisk, WSFNR and Georgia Student Chapter, American Fisheries Society; Adam Speir, WSFNR Student Chapter SWCS, and Lisa D'Amico, Soil and Water Conservation Society; Lt. Demetrius "Deek" Cox, USNR, for Xi Chapter of Xi Sigma Pi; Dr. Todd Rasmussen, WSFNR, for the history and logo of Georgia Student Chapter, American Water Resources Association.

On another history project, I had the pleasure to first make the acquaintance of Steven A. Brown, head of the University of Georgia Archives and Records Management. He was very helpful then and first mentioned he knew Dean Akerman's papers were deposited at the University of Virginia. On this present task, Steven has been a life saver. On my several visits to the Ilah Dunlap Little Memorial Library Hargrett Rare Book Room, Steven and his wonderful, professional staff have been extremely helpful and gracious. I'm sure I am not the typical "scholar" they are used to dealing with, but I was made to feel at home anyway. Each time I visited, Steven had everything I needed researched, sorted, and waiting for me to peruse. What a pleasure it was. Thanks, Steven!

I certainly pestered Carla Rapp, Tim Lowrimore, and Alva Hopkins of the GFA staff enough to probably lose my Fresh Air Barbeque rights. Thanks, guys, for all you did. To my friend and forestry classmate Joe Allen, Southeastern Wood Producers Association, thanks for the friendship, encouragement and help on the Logger of the Year listing. Special thanks to my former Executive Assistant Carol McCoy for her eagle-eye proofing and to Chad Galloway for his editing expertise. Here at the Warnell School, I owe Mary McCormack, Jenny Yearwood, Bridget Harden, J. P. Bond, Barbara Trotter, Gail Lebengood, and Eugene MacIntyre for putting up with my sometimes incessant whining for help in prying out some arcane (and probably useless) bit of information, musty book, or faded photograph. Also, special thanks are in order for Cecil Jennings, Steve Castleberry, Larry Morris, Aaron Fisk, and Adam Speir for their dogged help in rounding up the histories of the various student clubs and units in the School of Forestry and Natural Resources. Helen Fosgate, formerly of the School and now with the Georgia Department of Natural Resources Wildlife Resources Division, is especially to blame for making the initial approach to me to see if I would attempt writing this book, but she was extremely helpful in gathering old files and photographs. Kudos to Rachel G. Schneider, USFS, who supplied the historical leadership tenure for the U.S. Forest Service's Chattahoochee and Oconee National Forests. Bill Consoletti provided updated information on the Society of American Foresters.

Special thanks are due Dr. Richard A. LaFleur, UGA Franklin Professor of Classics, for the Latin translation. *Salve*, Rick.

For Dick Porterfield and Steve McWilliams I am truly thankful for your help and cheerful encouragement to "write one for the forestry Gipper." Thanks for your confidence in me and my ability to remember back to 1905. It was tough, guys.

I want to single out Steve Anderson, Forest History Society, for a special thank you. Steve provided personal encouragement and proofed the manuscript. He renders a great service to forestry in his job. My special thanks to Forest History Society Visiting Scholar Jamie Lewis for his insightful critique.

For my special friends who lent an empathetic ear and provided help whenever I asked, I am much obliged. Chuck Leavell, the "Rock and Roll Tree Farmer," was unselfish enough to write the Foreword while heavily involved in the Stones' "A Bigger Bang Tour." He is the definition of "servant leader." Thanks, Chuck, rock on. My friends and former professors, Reid Parker and Klaus Steinbeck, got calls late at night or early in the morning regarding some fact I had to have. They were always kind enough not to remember how stupid I was as a student and tried to help me along and not just to get rid of me. Track star Fred Haeussler patiently responded to my many requests for information on our national SAF presidents from Georgia, long-forgotten names and dates related to UCC and the university. Scott Jones, one of our most talented young alumni, was a bulldog in getting me some Forest Landowner Association material. Dr. Sven-Eric Appelroth, Finnish Forest Research Institute, has been encouraging and offered his usual highly philosophical but dirt-practical advice on how I should approach this work. Keep that *lurlu* going for me, Sven-Eric; I'll get back one of these days. My close forester friends, Bill Oettmeier, Jr., and Frankie Riley, Jr., have hunted down all manner of detail for me without too much racket in its course. Bill, I surely never did see that big buck on Izlar Road, and Frank, I can do a rolling fly cast—really.

I am especially indebted to Joyce Black, Tina Jones, and Morgan Nolan. They made it happen. Joyce was always there to correct my mistakes with word processing, make copies, and keep me straight in general. Tina efficiently did a prodigious amount of typing and collating various documents with never anything but a cheerful smile. I'm sure Morgan wonders how I ever made it out of the nineteenth century and into the twenty-first. She has been ever so efficient in helping me gather well over 1,300 photographs and cull them down to the few you see here. She did the scanning, finagling, storing, sorting, and printing of all the images and much more. Thank you, ladies!

I have borrowed shamelessly and often from those who wrote it better and knew it better. Of course, they deserve the credit for their efforts and not me. So, for the folks whose works I've relied on heavily—the late Dr. Andrew M. Soule, Bonnell Stone, Dean Gordon Marckworth, "Profs" Grant and Bishop, Drs. Hargreaves and Campbell and the live Leon Brown — thanks very much for blazing such an easy cruise line to follow. Just so everybody knows up front, I have particularly leaned on *Seventy-Five Years Service* (I've officially listed the author as the School of Forest Resources, although I suspect Buddy Hargreaves wrote it, but nobody remembers), Bonnell H. Stone's 1923 *The Georgia Forestry Association*, and Leondus Brown's 1982 *75 Years of GFA—An Anniversary Special* for the backbone of this book. Without their scholarship, I could not have finished the job. They gave great help, and I have gratefully listed them as "contributors." However, as author, I accept full responsibility for any errors, omissions, misstatements of fact or otherwise stupid, egregious mistakes I should have known about or better of. The turn of logs stops here.

This is not my magnum opus. That would be my family, friends, and any lives I may have somehow influenced positively. Janice, Tate, Joel, Edna, and Mikey: I give thanks to the Lord for your love.

Introduction

Georgia natural pine stand at sunrise. *Courtesy GFA*

A Journey of Partners

So, this book is the tale of the journey Georgia forestry has taken over a hundred years. It is a story of the University of Georgia Warnell School of Forestry and Natural Resources and the organization that immediately grew out of it, the Georgia Forestry Association. It is a daunting challenge to try to do adequate justice to both organizations. Yet, it is a remarkable story of how these two groups have had such a positive effect on resource conservation. How did the School and Association develop as they did?

The journey is intertwined between the school and its graduates, the Association and its members, and the critical influence they all have had on forestry not only in Georgia but throughout the South, the nation, and the world. Too often we learn little of history, and so all too often every generation makes the same mistakes. But just maybe, the leaders produced by the School and Association have had better vision, finer wisdom, and the courage of conviction to correct past mistakes and truly learn and change.

It is fitting that the South's oldest forestry school (1906) was established at the nation's oldest state-chartered university (1785). One year later, the South's oldest continuously operating forestry association was founded by people of vision and concern at the time for our dwindling forest resources. The journey they have made together has not been without a lot of racket in its course. Their journey is one that started in the lulling pools of hope and imagination and went through crashing shoals of bitter reality. In the literally reams of papers, books, manuscripts, minutes, magazines, pamphlets, news articles, letters, account sheets, scholarly works, broadsheets, working papers, and who knows what else that were reviewed in researching this book; there is a harsh story of both organizations starting strong and then getting moved, renamed, reorganized, going dormant, being severely affected by wars and bad economic times, and somehow making it through. Through all of this, the School and Association never lost their strategic vision, and they stuck to their purpose. Perhaps that is why they have had such a profound, positive influence. It has been all about the good people involved and sterling leadership.

A Story of Relationships

One of the many things that has been so amazing about this mutual journey is the personal friendships and relationships that are woven throughout the last hundred years. It is not just the friendship of Hill and Peabody, but that of Akerman and Stone, the Oettmeiers and Langdales, Hargreaves and Lufburrow, Grant and Shirley, Yearwood and Lancaster, Jones, and the Gillises, Patterson and Talmadge, Killorin, and Binns, and so many others who made things happen. Those friendships were born in the classroom and forged on the battlefield or boardroom. They worked.

A simple but striking example of this is retold by the late Dr. Charlie Fitzgerald, Forestry Class of 1942, who taught silviculture at the School for many years. Forestry School friendships transcended rank in WWII. Sgt. Fitzgerald went into a PX canteen with several officers who were his classmates. There was no saluting, just fond remembrance. "Perhaps this was the first time I realized the value and depth of old college friendships,"[1] he said.

He mentioned that Professor "Bish" Grant obtained for him an interview with Georgia-Pacific's Owen Cheatum and Bob Pamplin. He and Carl Stelling are supposed to be the first two graduate foresters hired by G-P. "As a group, we proved the value of the professional forester for generations to follow. I'm proud of this—we made it."[2] As a professor at Georgia, Fitzgerald summed up his love of the profession and passed it on to others with this: "…I sincerely hope that I have given some of my experience and knowledge to the next generation. I've never forgotten what my preceding generation did for me."[3]

The structure of this book is a separate history for the School of Forestry and Natural Resources and Georgia Forestry Association blended into the context of what was happening in forestry at the time. It was easier to do it this way rather than try to weave their histories together by time period. The Appendices contain important but ancillary material about both groups, Georgia Forestry and, of course, the Champions of Forestry profiles.

So, this is a long, amazing journey that has profoundly changed the course of conservation in Georgia and many parts of the world. The professors, students, graduates, professionals, loggers, truck drivers, secretaries, forest landowners, and friends have labored together for a common good higher than any one of them. The people of Georgia have benefited immensely for generations past and for those to come. The journey has been exciting and rewarding.

'Neath The Pine Trees' Stately Shadow[1]

Dwindling Forest Conditions

The 1924 *Forestry Almanac* estimated Georgia's original forest cover at a fully stocked 36,480,000 acres or almost the entire land area of the state.[2] Things were not so spectacular in 1900. Harold Brown quoted Dr. Harold Nix of the University of Georgia saying that idyllic farm life "…is mostly an urban myth, created by people who are harried by city traffic but have never sweated to make crops grow or put in sixteen hours on a dilapidated tractor under a hot South Georgia sun." Brown put the reality of farm life in focus. The "lack of education and lack of means" were two very strong causes of the horrible degradation of Georgia's farm and forest lands in the early twentieth century.[3]

Gayther Plummer reported the following forest situation in Georgia between 1910 and 1920, when forest cover was at a historic low: "At that time about 87% of the Piedmont was, or had been, cultivated."[4] The conversion from forests to agriculture in Georgia had this effect: "…nearly all the original topsoil was lost from 47 percent of the uplands, and gullying was apparent on 44 percent of the piedmont."[5]

Opposite page: Picnicking on a yellow poplar stump in Morgan County, 1915.
Courtesy Charles Mason & WSFNR

Virgin longleaf at the turn of the nineteenth century. *Courtesy Ted Walker/USFS*

Chopping a box, 1901. This turpentine method was very destructive. Photo taken by C. H. Herty. *Courtesy Ted Walker/USFS*

Pete Gerrell has done an excellent job in describing the forestry and logging conditions in the South in the late 1800s and early 1900s in his well-illustrated book. In 1903 Georgia sawmill stumpage was estimated to be $12 million.[6] He describes the early large size trees that were so tempting during the "cut out and get out" era of logging in the late 1800s and early 1900s. The early forest must have been a wonder to see. What sawmiller would not salivate upon seeing trees like those described by Plummer:

> *The original pine trees yielded square-sawn timbers 40–70 feet long, clear of knots, commonly 12–16 inches in diameter at the small end and 18–28 inches diameter at the large end with 190–200 rings per 10–11 inches radius, of which about 2 inches was sapwood, and yielded 450–900 feet of lumber.[7]*

Those virgin forest conditions did not last long. The forests of South Georgia were so open in the 1910s you could see a white mule a mile away.[8] The two biggest problems facing forestry in South Georgia at the beginning of the twentieth century were piney woods rooters and fire. Semi-wild pigs ranged freely through the forests and wiregrass, damaging seedlings and saplings. As Mart Stewart explained, "Even when longleaf pines were able to reseed themselves, hogs sometimes made short work of both seeds and seedlings."[9]

THE CENTENNIAL HISTORY OF FORESTRY IN GEORGIA

Turn-of-the-century Georgia was not what we see today. War, poor agricultural practices and just plain sorry logging had blighted the land. Tom Reed, longtime University of Georgia registrar, was a great chronicler of Georgia. Here is what he had to say about the forest conditions when the University was little more than one hundred years old:

> Throughout that century [nineteenth century] Georgia had magnificent forests, but little attention was given either to their preservation or improvement. They furnished lumber for construction of houses, and the naval stores industry had been built up, but methods of utilizing the output of Georgia forests were generally crude and wasteful.[10]

The box method of hacking out a resin reservoir at the base of large gum-producing pines was certainly destructive and wasteful. "Boxed" trees tended to topple, were highly susceptible to fire, and were inefficient gum producers. Charles Holmes Herty (see "Champions of

Typical southern wildfire destruction, ca. 1910s. *Courtesy WSFNR*

Forestry" profile) began investigating a new method of gum production for the Bureau of Forestry.

Herty published his research findings on his cup-and-gutter system in 1903 in a Bureau of Forestry bulletin. This treatise bluntly stated the naval stores industry was in critical condition because:

> Until recently the destructive methods (the box system) in use have been regarded with entire indifference in the regions affected. This has been due to the low valuation of timber throughout the turpentine belt, and to the popular belief that the pine forests of the Southern States were inexhaustible. But it has now become evident that if the naval-stores industry is to be perpetuated, some method must be found which will not be prohibitive of later operations in the same field.[11]

His bulletin went on to detail the "evils" of the destructive chopped box gum-gathering system as well as the merits of the clay cup-and-gutter method. After many years of experiments, he noted the success of his work because new gum leases were only being granted if the operators ensured the use of his system.[12, 13]

New face with Herty cup, ca. 1930s. *Courtesy Ted Walker/ USFS*

At the beginning of the twentieth century the mood of the nation was one of great concern and even alarm about the state of our forest resources. In 1905, the American Forestry Association organized the American Forest Congress in Washington, D.C., "…to establish a broader understanding of the forest in its relation to the great

Railroad logging in "cut out and get out" era, ca. early 1900s. *Courtesy Ted Walker/USFS*

Overhead steam skidder of Hebard Lumber Company in the Okefenokee Swamp, 1909. *Courtesy Bob Izlar*

Typical erosion problems caused by indiscriminate harvesting in the Southern Appalachians, ca. 1920s. *Courtesy WSFNR*

Above: Early public relations poster on the danger of forest fires, ca. 1930s. *Courtesy WSFNR*

Below: Log train near Ocilla, Georgia, ca. early 1900s. *Courtesy Ted Walker and Bob Izlar*

industries depending on it...to stimulate and unite all efforts to perpetuate the forest as a permanent resource of the nation."[14]

A Rising Tide of Concern

At the 1905 American Forest Congress, President Teddy Roosevelt gave the opening address and set the tone of the event:

> *It always takes time to get the mind of a people accustomed to any change in conditions, and it took a long time to get the mind of our people, as a whole, accustomed to the fact that they had to alter their attitude toward the forests. For the first time the great business and forest interests of the nation have joined together...to consider their individual and their common interests in the forest.*[15]

At the Congress, Dr. Lawton Wiggins, vice chancellor of the University of the South in Tennessee, addressed the question, "What should be the attitude of our universities toward forestry?"[16] He was a southerner, and Sewanee's domain was the largest forested campus in the nation at the time.[17] He started answering the question with, "There is no profession I know of that requires wider knowledge than does forestry."[18] He felt a university environment and not a separate school, like the Biltmore Forest School, was the best place for forestry education because a forester handling practical problems needed the broadening experience of different viewpoints. Wiggins set out this challenge for the type of person a university should produce:

> *We need him to solve our fire problem and devise means for prevention of and protection from this arch enemy of forest management. His scientifically established facts regarding tree growth, influences, and value present and future will strengthen our pleas to state legislatures for wisely conceived far-sighted tax laws."* (Author's emphasis)[19]

Based on his positive experience at the American Forest Congress, President Teddy Roosevelt convened the White House Conference of Governors in 1908. This helped signal an increased national focus on natural resource conservation.[20] The stage was set for momentous things in Georgia.

The whisper of the crosscut "gator tail" saw was soon supplanted by the roar of the chain saw, ca. 1920s.
Courtesy WSFNR/USFS

Superior Pine Products Company firefighting crew in Suwannee Forest, Fargo, Georgia, 1929. The pine tops work if you know how. *Courtesy Ted Walker/USFS*

The Right Three

Georgia forestry was blessed by the friendship of three men in the right place at the right time—George Foster Peabody, University Chancellor Walter B. Hill, and Chancellor David C. Barrow. In discussing Chancellors Hill and Barrow, one must conclude they knew it was all about leadership. They were determined that the University of Georgia would lead the way. There was no teaching of forestry in the state other than a small reference in some College of Agriculture courses. In fact, in the University's early years, students were forbidden to go more than a mile off campus. Tom Reed noted, "… if they [the students] ever saw forests or walked through them, it was when they were home or on their vacation, and even then they were not carefully and effectively studied as to their real value, their protection from fire or their conservation and improvement."[21]

University Chancellor Walter B. Hill saw the need for improving the forest condition in Georgia, and he determined the University of Georgia could do it.

Hill was good friends with George Foster Peabody, a Georgia-born New York philanthropist. According to Reed, Peabody was a "willing listener and enthusiastic helper" who became "thoroughly convinced of the usefulness" of a forestry school to the University.[22] As an Athens houseguest of the Hodgson family around 1900, Peabody became acquainted with the University of Georgia and its needs. He was made a life trustee of the University. He quickly sought to help the College of Agriculture by buying adjacent farm land for it. He even financed two train excursions to the University of Wisconsin and Cornell so Georgia policymakers could see firsthand how the best agricultural schools operated. On these trips, he hosted the governor, University officials, leading legislators, the news media, and wives.[23]

Peabody became the School's benefactor, offering the University trustees $2,000 per year for three years and $500 per year for expenses. The money was to be used to establish a school of forestry and hire a professor of forestry.[24] The offer was made by letter on November 15,

Savannah, Georgia, rosin yard, ca. 1920s. Note wooden barrels, which were later replaced by galvanized ones. *Courtesy Ted Walker/USFS*

Pole trailer with cypress logs, ca. 1930s. *Courtesy Ted Walker/USFS*

1905.[25] However, before it was accepted by the trustees in April 1906, Chancellor Hill died. Yet, there was no need to despair; as Reed noted, "The guidance of the new school could not have been given to a greater lover of forests than David C. Barrow."[26]

Here are a few quotes from Reed that describe the new Chancellor Barrow's feeling about forestry:

> Against the prodigal waste and careless handling of our forests he was always protesting. His voice was one of the earliest in Georgia crying out against such habits on the part of landowners. And on his own farms he practiced what he preached.[27] . . .We vote bonds and pass them on to the next generation. Why not plant trees and pass them on as an offset?[28] . . . He at all times sought to impress on owners of timber lands the necessity of informing themselves of the real value of timber. He was satisfied that landowners, as a rule, had no idea of the value of the timber they sold and didn't believe the average buyer had much more idea of the value of timber he bought.[29]

So, Barrow was a champion of forestry and a strong proponent of the newly endowed school. Reed noted, "The forest had great fascination for Mr. Barrow. It is doubtful whether, aside from his fellow-men, he loved anything quite so much as a tree."[30]

Dean Gordon Marckworth offered this summary of the beginnings of the School:

> This offer was accepted by the Board and the School was established as "The George Foster Peabody School of Forestry." At the meeting of the trustees in April, 1906, Mr. Alfred Akerman, then State Forester of Massachusetts, was elected Professor of Forestry, and was to begin his duties on the first of July.
>
> In June Mr. Peabody proposed to make a donation of $500 annually for three years, provided the State would donate not less than $1,000 additional annually for three years, to be spent, under the direction of the Professor of Forestry, "for investigating the forestry problems of the State and promoting the perpetuation and proper management of the forests therein." So far as the available records show, this offer was not accepted and only the original sum was made available.[31]

Alfred A. Akerman, a native of Georgia born in 1876, was a Georgia graduate in the Class of 1898 with a B.A. degree and an M.F. degree from Yale. He was recruited to the School from his post as Massachusetts state forester. He also had been Connecticut state forester briefly.[32]

In his last official report to the Massachusetts legislature as state forester, he stated his reasons for taking up the Georgia offer:

> In April I was elected to the chair of Forest Engineering in the University of Georgia, one branch of which [Franklin College] I am a graduate. My reasons for accepting the professorship were explained in a note to the Governor, as follows: "I do not leave the Commonwealth because of dissatisfaction with my work; on the contrary, I have enjoyed my service here as only one can who loves to fight for a good cause. Nor does the place in Georgia carry a larger salary; but I believe that it offers a better opportunity to forward the cause for which we foresters are working, and I feel it my duty to go."[33]

Peabody's vision and the strong personal support of two university chancellors[34] led to the establishment of an institution that would foster the development of another similar in purpose but different in organization and action. With the establishment of the School, Dean Akerman was in the right place to accomplish much good. He realized the need to have an outside but close support group like the Georgia Forestry Association. Therefore, he founded the Georgia Forestry Association to be an advocate for the School. Thus began a century-long partnership of mutual help. These actions were the beginnings of progress in Georgia forest conservation.

Chancellor Barrow noted two things had to be accomplished: (1) stop the destruction of timber and (2) plant barren land. He felt the forest would recover if these things happened: "The opportunity for growing woods in Georgia is unsurpassed. Good timber will grow itself anywhere in the state."[35]

Influence for a Proper Understanding[1]

A man that devotes his life to learning, shall he not be learned?—Sir Thomas Carlyle

Starting the Job

The Department of Forestry[2] was inaugurated in the University Chapel on November 27, 1906, with Chancellor David C. Barrow presiding and the principal address given by Alfred Gaskin of the U.S. Forest Service on "The Progress of Forestry in the United States."[3] Dean Gordon Marckworth reported on Gaskin's speech that night:

> His address dealt with the progress of forestry in the United States and in closing he spoke of the part the school could play in the furtherance of forestry, particularly in Georgia. His words in this connection can well bear repeating for they apply as much today as they did then when he said "I sincerely hope that the establishment of a Forestry School in Georgia means more than an opportunity for your young men to become professional foresters. There should flow from this institution an influence for the proper understanding of the objects of forestry that shall be felt all over the State."

Opposite page: School of Forestry and Natural Resources, 1956. *Courtesy WSFNR*

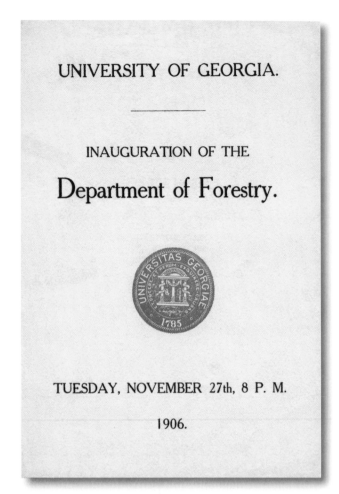

UNIVERSITY OF GEORGIA.

INAUGURATION OF THE

Department of Forestry.

TUESDAY, NOVEMBER 27th, 8 P. M.

1906.

Top: Dedication program for Department of Forestry, 1906. *Courtesy WSFNR*

Bottom: Hunt Griffin (center) and some of his friends in Summer Camp, Alachua, Florida (1909 or 1910). *Courtesy WSFNR*

In inaugurating the school it was not the purpose of the University, at that time, to prepare men for the profession of forestry. As stated in the University catalogue, issued April 1906: "While the University does not offer complete technical instruction to those who wish to prepare for professional practice, it is hoped that the courses offered will interest some to take up forestry as their life work, and will prepare them for the pursuit of their studies in the technical schools of forestry in this and foreign countries, and that they will return to contribute to the betterment of forestry conditions in Georgia. A series of investigations into forest problems of the State is being planned. As far as practical the students in both courses (Economics of Forestry, and, Practical Forestry) will assist in these investigations."[4]

A university setting was the place for a forestry school. Ernest Bruncken noted in 1900 that the need for a broader human understanding was "…why the training of a forester at college should not be a narrowly technical one. For a broad, liberal culture is the best basis for a deep and comprehensive insight into the ways of men of all classes."[5] While the University may not have originally intended on a degree course in forestry, the School's first proposed degree was a B.S. in Forest Engineering,[6] and Dean Alfred A. Akerman professed to be in a chair of forest engineering.

The School was first housed in Terrell Hall.[7] The new School had one room, a few books and chairs, and no students.[8] Waddell Hall, built in 1820–21, was known as Agricultural Hall from 1903 to 1909 and was the second home of the School.[9]

The University of Georgia Library Estrays collection has several of Dean Akerman's handwritten or typed annual reports from 1907 until he left in 1914. They provide an interesting glimpse into what he thought was important to report on progress. In 1907 his expenses were $593.55, and he called for expansion of the School's land and full control of it.[10] Expenses were considerably more in the next year at more than $8,000.[11]

Much was happening just two years after the School's inauguration.[12] He noted an effort would be made to create a "State Forester's Office," or a Board of Forestry. Yet, he was concerned that the public education work in forestry would be left to the School. To illustrate that concern, he reported quite candidly that he was assigned, without consultation, as superintendent of forestry for the eleven district school systems in Georgia.

He was also tasked to teach algebra and accounting. He admitted to being a poor math student in his days at University of Georgia Franklin College of Arts and Sciences. To keep ahead of the students, he took night

Top: "Grub-pile!" Professor Akerman eating with forestry class, 1910. *Courtesy WSFNR*

Bottom: Early forestry class, ca. 1915. Note Germanic clothing style. *Courtesy WSFNR*

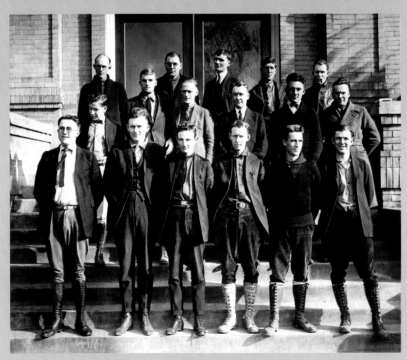

courses at the Athens Business College, and he lamented the golden opportunity that the university was missing by not having a business college.

Perhaps to bolster his position on staffing and teaching load, he appended three letters of endorsement for the summer camp from Henry Solon Graves, director of the Yale Forest School; Gifford Pinchot, chief of the U.S. Forest Service, and Dr. Charles H. Herty.

Moving under Agriculture

In the 1908 report, Akerman mentions his support of the transfer of the "Forest School" to the College of Agriculture and Mechanic Arts. The Division of Forestry was transferred to the Georgia State College of Agriculture and Mechanic Arts in 1907 by action of Chancellor Barrow and approval of the General Board of Trustees of the University. The first rooms for the division were in Lumpkin House. They moved to Barrow Hall, home of Agricultural Engineering, when it was completed in 1911.[13]

The main building of the College of Agriculture, Conner Hall, was built in 1908, and classes were held there beginning in 1909. It was modeled on Townsend Hall at Ohio State University. The Georgia State College of Agriculture and Mechanic Arts was established in 1859 as a part of the University of Georgia, but it had its own Board of Trustees, who in turn reported to the University of Georgia General Board of Trustees. The dean of the College was also its president. Perhaps the difference was most prominent in 1918 when women were admitted to the College of Agriculture two full years before the university did so. The president of the College of Agriculture was Andrew Soule, who was also known as "King Andy" for his overbearing management style.

Surveying class, ca. 1920s. *Courtesy WSFNR*

Akerman's last term was the 1913–14 academic year. There were thirty-eight students enrolled. The School had some sample plots in Madison County partly funded by Akerman. He did Extension work that year at Berry College, Nacoochee Institute, and Young Harris.

An Advisory Board was established, consisting of John M. Slaton, Henry S. Graves, James H. Baird, Frank E. Shippen, Augustus O. Dozier, and Bailey F. Williamson. They had experience in the law, forestry education, hardwood lumbering, local logging, and naval stores. Akerman also mentions a 320-acre arboretum in Towns County.[16]

In spring 1909, the curriculum was expanded, and the degree course in forestry was offered.[17] The first bachelor of science degree in forestry in the South was awarded to Josiah Tattnall Kollack in 1912.[18]

Dean Akerman resigned in 1914 and was replaced by James B. Berry, a graduate of the University of Minnesota.[19] Despite Akerman's earlier published support of the transfer of the department into the State College of Agriculture, he became very dissatisfied with Dean Andrew Soule and tendered his resignation in 1912, but Chancellor Barrow dissuaded him from leaving.[20] Finally, things came to a head, and Akerman blamed his leaving on Soule, noting, "The College is concerned more with things that appeal to numbers and that make more of a showing."[21]

Top: School nursery at Oconee Forest, 1932. *Courtesy WSFNR*

Bottom: Burley M. Lufburrow (on right with slice of bread) visits a logging camp at mealtime, ca. mid-1920s. *Courtesy Ted Walker/USFS*

In 1911 seventy-six students were enrolled. Summer camp was held in Alachua, Florida, at a cost of $45.84 per student. Akerman made a plea for more staff.[14]

For his 1912 annual report, Akerman noted, "In trying to build up a forest school here I have not been greatly concerned about there not being many students to take the courses; for I have felt that the students would come if we gave good courses." He asked for an additional staff forester. There were eight students in the degree track course. Summer camp was replaced by sawmill work and a written report.[15]

The Forestry Cabin in winter, ca. 1920s. *Courtesy WSFNR*

CHILDS, MINEAR, CARRUTH, EBERHARDT

Top: Forestry class in the late 1920s. *Courtesy WSFNR*

Bottom: 1936 Summer Camp, Olustee, Florida. *Courtesy WSFNR*

Soule announced the start of a forest nursery for Georgia. His expectation was an initial production of 500,000 trees. Species produced at the nursery were slash, longleaf, and loblolly pines. The seedlings were sold for $3 a thousand and were recommended to be planted at 900 trees per acre. Soule said planned nursery production was 5 million seedlings per year, or enough to reforest 500,000 acres.[22]

The first School nursery, which contained native species as well as ornamentals and basket willows, was established on the present-day site of Sanford Stadium in the 1916–17 school year and was in production until

1928, when it was moved to the Oconee Forest and eventually abandoned in 1942.[23, 24]

The School was authorized by the graduate school to grant graduate degrees in forestry in 1917. However, the first master of science in forestry degree was not awarded until 1932.[25, 26]

The Interwar Years

The Department of Forestry became involved in the war effort in 1918 as a Student Army Training Corps. The program, sponsored by the War Department, consisted of a two-year technical course in forest engineering. At war's end, the School provided vocational education, known as "rehabilitation," to returning veterans by offering two two-year courses for forest rangers.[27]

Much of the idealism of the conservation movement ended with the disillusionment that followed the "Great War," when Thomas D. Burleigh became division head in 1920.[28] Despite the slump in conservation activity, the Division of Forestry had increased to sixteen students and three professors by 1924. The Forestry Club became very active with publication of the first *Cypress Knee* that year. This publication lasted until 1972. The name referred to something unique to southern forestry.

A log cabin was also built in 1924—entirely by hand—by members of the Forestry Club. Each afternoon, students who didn't have classes worked from noon to dark until the structure was completed. The fact that the log cabin lasted until 1956 before it finally rotted beyond repair attests to the builders' skill.[29, 30] Its granite chimney still remains.

Summer camp was held in various places from Fannin County to Alachua County, Florida, to Towns, Greene, and Clinch Counties.[31, 32, 33] At least one early camp had a mascot—a skunk.[34]

The years following World War I saw a change in attitudes toward traditional male roles. Forestry was no exception—Jane Oakley enrolled as the first female forestry student in 1924. However, she did not graduate. The first woman to graduate, Pat Holbrook, did so in 1969. The excellence of the postwar student body was recognized on February 16, 1926, with the establishment of the Gamma Chapter of Alpha Xi Sigma, Forestry

Honor Society. This society remained active until the beginning of World War II.[35]

A 1926 *Forestry Almanac* article on the Division of Forestry noted the School had four aims: "…instruction in economics of forestry; instruction in the practical elements of forestry to aid agricultural students; theoretical and practical work for students planning to make it their profession, and popular education throughout the State."

Courses offered were: fundamentals of forestry, farm forestry, dendrology, silviculture, forest protection, mensuration and management, lumbering, utilization, wood technology, sawmill construction and mechanics, forest drawing, and surveying. Juniors and seniors took courses for intense specialization. Twenty-five students were enrolled for the 1925–26 academic year. Faculty members were: Thomas D. Burleigh, associate professor of forestry; Leslie E. Sawyer, adjunct professor, and DuPre Barrett, Extension specialist in forestry.[36]

The year 1929 is most often remembered for the Stock Market Crash and the beginning of the Great Depression.

Right: Another Sunday afternoon at the cabin, ca. early 1930s. Courtesy WSFNR

Below: A class from the late 1930s posing behind Conner Hall. Courtesy WSFNR

Funding was almost nonexistent, and like many state-supported institutions, the Division of Forestry fell on extremely lean times.

Interest in forestry was so meager in the early years that the School's continued existence was uncertain. By 1930 the situation was changed, with Dean Soule crowing about it being one of his best degree programs and of excellent relations with the U.S. Forest Service and other state and national agencies. The School then had three instructors and two Extension agents. He felt the graduates of 1930 would be able to provide leadership to "…re-organize the forest interests of Georgia along wise, efficient, and essential economic lines."[37]

Soule saw the worth of the School in benefiting the taxpayers:

Above: A class from the 1930s. *Courtesy WSFNR*

Right: Senior student Harley Langdale, Jr., leader of the Student Revolt of '37, 1936. *Courtesy WSFNR*

Far right: Famous pamphlet paid for by students to publicize the Revolt of '37. *Courtesy WSFNR*

DO YOU KNOW?

1. Present Rating of School of Forestry by Society of American Foresters.

2. The History of the School of Forestry.

3. The Actual Conditions as They Exist at Present.

4. The Need for an Accredited School of Forestry in Region 8.

5. What Can Be Done.

Sponsored and Paid for by

THE STUDENT BODY

The newspaper clipping (image 1) contains the following text:

SEPTEMBER, 1956   2

From Then . . . 'Til Now
History Of Peabody Forestry School

A handful of students interested in a new and little-known profession gathered together in a modest little house in 1906 in Athens, Ga. That was the beginning of the George Foster Peabody School of Forestry.

Since then, the school has evolved into a modern well-equipped institution that has assumed leadership in the nation's vital forest industry. Hundreds of young men have filed through its classrooms to take their places in highly-skilled

Barrow Hall

positions throughout the forests of the world.

The University of Georgia had existed for more than a hundred years when the noted educational philanthropist George Foster Peabody donated funds in 1905 for establishing a forestry program at the school. To initiate the program, Alfred Akerman, the school's first Professor of Forestry, met with a small group of interested students in the future home of the late T. W. Reed. The curriculum was somewhat limited in the beginning. Only nine courses were taught,

Reese House

including dendrology, protection, silviculture, forest economics, lumbering management and farm forestry. Each student worked for the newly created Bachelor of Science in Forest Engineering degree. Ultimate aims of the course were to encourage appreciation of forests, to teach forest management, to acquaint the student with techniques of lumbering and forest engineering and to encourage forestry education throughout the state.

Although the school offered a surprisingly broad program in the early years, it was hastily pointed out that students should "distinctly understand" that the limited facilities of the University could not offer complete instruction in the forestry profession. Students were advised not to practice forestry until they supplemented their training by one or two years of special preparation at an institution offering post graduate instruction in forest engineering.

Enrollment continued to be small because of the relative novelty of the course and because forestry as a profession still was too new to arouse much interest. Only five or six students comprised the school's entire enrollment, although at one time there were only eight scattered throughout the four-year course.

Limitations of confining forestry instruction to the classroom were realized at an early date. In 1909, two summer terms

Plant Pathology Building

were added to the curriculum. The summer terms were divided into two camps. The first was held in the lumbering center of North Georgia, and the second in the longleaf belt of South Georgia and Florida. Object of the camps was to acquaint the students with camp life and afford an opportunity of studying various forestry activities in diverse areas.

When the State College of Agriculture was reorganized in 1907, the Division of Forestry

(Continued on Page 9)

Left of dotted line shows proposed wing to present Forestry Building

Homes of the Warnell School of Forestry and Natural Resources through time, including the "dog house" (Plant Pathology), 1956. *Courtesy Georgia Forestry Commission*

Our Division of Forestry is undoubtedly creating a new consciousness in the minds of our people relative to the growth of trees and the necessity of protecting the same. . . . It is also being made manifest that if fire is kept out of our forest areas and the trees judiciously thinned, they will provide the farmers [sic] with an income of much larger proportions than he was ever thought them capable of yielding. . . . In fact, our income from forests sources ought to be increased to a maximum of at least fifty million dollars a year beyond its present volume and kept there for an indefinite time.[38]

He said that there was an urgent need for a separate forestry building and that plans had been drawn for

a $100,000 building. This need had been recognized and anticipated by Professor Trowbridge in 1929.[39, 40]

Despite hard times, this era saw not only conservation, in the form of public works, reawakened in the public's mind but also several events important to the School of Forest Resources. In 1931 Gordon D. Marckworth replaced Burleigh as division head, and the first alumni newsletter was published as a joint project of Alpha Xi Sigma and the Forestry Club.[41, 42]

Independent...Again

In 1931 the Georgia General Assembly passed the Reorganization Act, which reorganized all state government agencies. It created the University System of Georgia Board of Regents. The new Board of Regents took over the previously independent Georgia State College of Agriculture and Mechanic Arts in 1933. There was a severe personality clash between University of Georgia President Sanford and State Agriculture College President Andrew "King Andy" Soule over this reorganization. Soule lost out and resigned. In 1935 the Board of

Dean Weddell and faculty, winter 1941. *Courtesy WSFNR*

Lumberjack Ball beauty contest, ca. late 1940s. *Courtesy WSFNR*

Regents authorized changing the Division of Forestry, College of Agriculture to the George Foster Peabody School of Forestry, and in 1936 the School was deeded the Whitehall Forest from the Georgia Rehabilitation Corporation.[43, 44]

Yale Dean Henry Graves wrote in the 1930 *Cypress Knee* about changes he saw in forestry education. He felt a forestry school should set itself apart by rendering "…some distinctive service for which it is specially qualified." He also noted the need, even back in 1930, that the concept of a forestry education must be broadened beyond silviculture and "technical management."[45] In a 1935 national report on forestry education by the Society of American Foresters (also know as the Chapman Report), Georgia was rated a "Class C" school, or the lowest rating possible.[46]

The Student Revolt of 1937

The Chapman Report noted the School of Forestry suffered from inadequate facilities and too small a faculty. The School was first accredited by the Society of American Foresters, in 1934. In the accreditation report, a shortcoming noted was the lack of adequate facilities. The report further stated plans were afoot to build "new facilities in two years."

Conditions at the School were in a fine mess in early 1937 when Professor Allyn M. Herrick resigned in disgust and left for Purdue. This resignation prompted a mass student meeting in the chapel to discuss the situation. There were threats of a student strike. President Caldwell tried to maintain calm by saying he would place a new building for the School on an emergency list for the Board of Regents. Senior forestry student Harley Langdale, Jr. (from south Georgia), and nine other forestry students went to see Governor E. D. "Ed" Rivers, who was from Lanier County in South Georgia. Downing Musgrove was Rivers' executive secretary, and he was from Homerville, also in South Georgia, so Langdale felt he at least had an audience of men with similar backgrounds. He recalled the governor told them, "What you boys should do is see the Board of Regents chairman." The student delegation went to see

Courtesy WSFNR

Forestry Club meeting on Fire Tower Hill, 1948. *Courtesy WSFNR*

him the same day and complained about no buildings, old books, treatment as outcasts in the old vet school "dog house" and the same "song and dance" they gave the governor. But they were flatly rejected. The Regents' chairman, Marion Smith, was angry that they even dared see him, and he phoned University President Harmon Caldwell. According to Langdale, the Regent hotly told Caldwell, "If boys like these ever worry me again, I'll resign as Chairman of the Board of Regents."[47]

When they returned to campus, they were hastily summoned to the president's office where they received an "official" scolding and were told never to do anything like that ever again. Yet, the subtle message they took away was, "You did the right thing, and I appreciate what you did."[48] The students published, at their expense, the now famous "Do You Know?" pamphlet that explained in detail the possible loss of accreditation, living in the "dog house," and salary and facility conditions. This call to action was distributed through-out the state.[49, 50]

The "student revolt of 1937" made headlines in the *Atlanta Journal Constitution* with a three-column article

March 28, 1937. The students complained the School was "in the dog house" because it was forced to take up shabby quarters in the building vacated by the recently closed Veterinary Medicine School.[51] After that, Executive Secretary Downing Musgrove (who was also a big forest landowner) helped to quietly move things along. Langdale notes this was the first time there was any legal consideration of the importance of timber to the state. Marckworth left in disgust over the lack of support and went to the University of Washington.[52]

Out of the "Dog House" and into War

After being bounced from Lumpkin Hall to Barrow Hall in 1911 and then in 1934 to the abandoned veterinary medicine building, the School of Forestry was finally settled in the present "Classic" Forestry Building in 1938, following the student revolt and hints on non-accreditation by the Society of American Foresters. The new building was considered one of the most beautiful on campus. It was completed September 1, 1938, at a cost of $120,000 with another $65,000 for equipment. The offices, halls, and classrooms were richly paneled in donated pecky cypress, knotty pine, heart red

Class of 1952.
Courtesy WSFNR

Lumberjack Ball at Bull of the
Woods Dance Hall, 1947.
Courtesy WSFNR

1956. *Courtesy WSFNR*

gum, white oak, cypress, and tupelo gum. A special niche was built to hold the bust of the School's namesake, George Foster Peabody.[53]

The "Program for the Presentation of the Bust of George Foster Peabody, April 27, 1939," gave a description of the bust:

> The bust was carved from life by Simon Moselsio of Bennington, Vermont. It was carved from an oak grown at Mr. Peabody's home "Yaddo" at Saratoga Springs, New York. It is presented to the School of Forestry by his daughter, Mrs. Marjorie Peabody Waite.[54]

For many years, students would toss pennies behind the bust for good luck during finals. When the Classic Building was extensively remodeled during the 1970s, the niche was plastered over, and the bust was moved to the Peabody Board Room of the UGA Henry W. Grady College of Journalism.

By 1940 the School was comfortably settled in the new building. That year, Donald J. Weddell became dean of forestry. His tenure would be marked by the war and a greatly reduced Forestry School, as most students and faculty went to war. It was to Dean Weddell's credit that the School survived the war years and was ready when the nation again discovered the value of the southern pine resource. Dean Weddell was faculty advisor to Blue

Key and Omicron Delta Kappa. He served as dean from 1939 until his death in 1956.

In 1941 with the help of Professor A. E. Patterson, the Gamma Chapter of Alpha Xi Sigma secured a charter from Xi Sigma Pi, and Alpha Xi Sigma ceased to exist at Georgia. The Xi Chapter financed the War Memorial plaque at the entrance to the original Forestry Building.[55]

The WWII years clearly had an effect on the School. Even the 1943 *Cypress Knee* was mimeographed. Dean Weddell's somber message in that issue noted timber sales to support various segments of the war effort and the fact that the School might have to close "for the duration."[56] The University was giving special dispensation to students being called into service. If students were within twenty-one hours of graduation, they were granted their degrees. It is sad to read through Dean Weddell's personal copy of that 1943 *Cypress Knee*. It listed a class roster for each graduating class back to the first graduate. He had annotated many names in pencil with "dead."

The Cypress Knee was suspended in 1944–45. In his 1946 *Cypress Knee* message, Dean Weddell noted that on a percentage basis, the School had more students in WWII and more gold stars on the Service Flag than any other school or college within the University.[57]

In 1942 the Navy preflight school took over the Forestry Building.[58] Little or no adjustments were made in the forestry curriculum for returning veterans, while other units on campus did have to make changes. Returning veterans expected to be treated differently than younger students because they were much more mature and battle hardened. During WWII, the Forestry Club was inoperative from 1942 to 1945.

In 1946 the Earl Jenkins Memorial Award was established to honor the memory of a Georgia forestry graduate killed on Luzon in 1945. On May 5, 1951, a bronze plaque was dedicated to the memory of forestry graduates killed in the Second World War. Since then, other plaques have been added for the Korean and Vietnam conflicts.[59]

Out of the Sapling Stage

The School's seventy-five-year history reviews the situation in the 1950s:

1906 **50** **1956**

Golden Anniversary Celebration

George Foster Peabody School Of Forestry

SCHOOL OF FORESTRY
University of Georgia

1906–1956

GOLDEN ANNIVERSARY

UNIVERSITY OF GEORGIA
Athens, Georgia

CLASS IN SAWMILLING

Left: Golden Anniversary Celebration brochure, 1956. *Courtesy WSFNR*

Above: Seaboard Air Line Railroad Company Forestry Bulletin honoring the School of Forestry faculty for the Golden Anniversary, 1956. *Courtesy WSFNR*

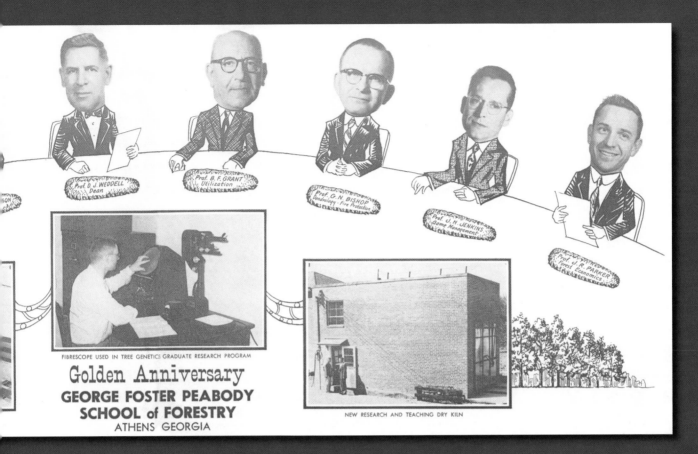

FIBRESCOPE USED IN TREE GENETICS GRADUATE RESEARCH PROGRAM

Golden Anniversary
**GEORGE FOSTER PEABODY
SCHOOL of FORESTRY**
ATHENS GEORGIA

NEW RESEARCH AND TEACHING DRY KILN

Prof. D. J. WEDDELL
Dean

Prof. B. F. GRANT
Utilization

Prof. G. N. BISHOP
Dendrology - Fire Protection

Prof. J. H. JENKINS
Game Management

Prof. J. R. PARKER
Forest Economics

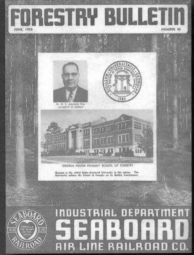

THE UNIVERSITY OF GEORGIA
THE GEORGE FOSTER PEABODY
SCHOOL OF FORESTRY
ATHENS, GEORGIA

ATHENS, GA.
SEP 1
8³⁰ AM
1956

1 GOLDEN ANNIVE
9 SCHOOL OF FOR S
0 UNIVERSITY OF
6

U.S. POSTAGE 3¢
LIBERTY

First day cancellation

Golden Anniversary congratulatory
Forestry Bulletin, 1956. *Courtesy
WSFNR*

Golden Anniversary first-day cancellation, 1956. *Courtesy WSFNR*

Above: School of Forestry and Natural Resources, 1956.
Courtesy WSFNR

Left: For many years, summer camp was held at Hard Labor
Creek State Park, 1956. *Courtesy WSFNR*

Seniors at work on final management maps, 1957. *Courtesy WSFNR*

With the 1950's, the Nation settled down to build new homes for the baby boom and enjoy the hard won victory. The demand for lumber, plywood and pulp increased harvesting of southern Yellow Pine that had reseeded following farm abandonment of the 20's and 30's. Industry, as well as State and Federal Government, began to realize that only through a vigorous program of regeneration would a "Third Forest" in the South be assured. This new interest in Forestry was reflected in increased activity in the Peabody School of Forestry. In 1950, the wildlife management curriculum was instituted through cooperation of the School of Forestry and the

Biology Department. The program offered a BSF with a major in wildlife management. The following year, the nursery at Whitehall was established. The faculty was expanded in 1954 and $100,000 was appropriated by the state for building restoration. In 1957 following the death of Dean Weddell, A. M. Herrick, the former professor who precipitated the 1938 [sic] student protest, was appointed dean. Under his twenty-four year tenure, the present School of Forest Resources developed.[60]

Dr. Jim Jenkins became the first wildlife management professor, in the early 1950s. The Ph.D. in forestry was authorized in 1963 and first awarded the following year to William R. Sizemore.[61] Forestry Buildings Two and Three were completed in 1967 and dedicated September 28, 1968, with U.S. Senator Herman Talmadge as keynoter.

The Board of Regents formally changed the name of the George Foster Peabody School of Forestry to the School of Forest Resources on January 10, 1968. Dean A. M. Herrick said the new name "… better describes the educational and research missions of the School.

Forestry Club initiation, 1957. *Courtesy WSFNR*

Above: Mr. and Mrs. Ace Parker practicing for conclave, 1957. *Courtesy WSFNR*

Left: Georgia Forest Research Council promotional brochure, ca. 1950s. *Courtesy WSFNR*

Whereas the emphasis originally was principally on timber management and administration, in more recent years other resources and amenities such as fish and game, forest recreation, watershed values and environmental quality have drawn increasing attention from foresters."[62]

Expanded Focus

On July 1, 1971, the School attained professional school status so students entered in their junior year. Of the nine southern schools with forestry courses, the one at the University of Georgia was known as the best.[63]

In 1976 the School's White Hall Mansion was restored with proceeds from the salvage sale of beetle-killed timber on Whitehall Forest. The School's recreational cabin, "Flinchum's Folly," burned in November 1977 but was rebuilt as "Flinchum's Phoenix" in April 1979. Fred Haeussler won a contest to name the reincarnation of "Flinchum's Folly." He submitted the name "Flinchum's Phoenix." According to ancient Greek mythology, the magical phoenix bird lived for 500 years, set itself on fire, then rose from its ashes to live for another five hundred years. Only one phoenix bird existed at a time. When the bird felt its death was near, it built a nest of aromatic wood, set it afire, and was consumed by the flames, only to rise again as a new bird. The symbol of the city of Atlanta is this same phoenix bird that signifies the city's resurgence from the flaming destruction of the Battle of Atlanta in the Civil War.

The students have long been active in extracurricular activities. The University of Georgia Forestry Club was founded February 4, 1914, by Professor Alfred Akerman as chairman and the seven students then enrolled in the

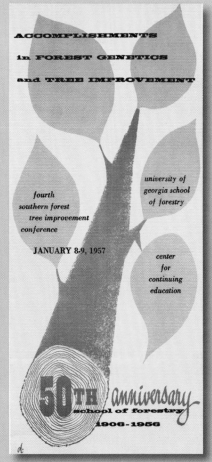

Left: "Accomplishments in Forest Genetics and Tree Improvement" brochure, 1957. *Courtesy WSFNR*

Above: Dr. Harry V. Wiant, Jr. (L), former master's student and future SAF national president, and Dr. Carmen learning "functional wiring" even before punch cards, 1959. *Courtesy Dr. Harry V. Wiant*

School. The club's all-time membership high was 180 in the 1948–49 academic year. The Forestry Club helped found the Association of Southern Forestry Clubs and hosted the first annual Conclave of Southeastern Forestry Schools on May 10, 1958, along with seven other schools at Rock Eagle.[64] Georgia has since hosted the conclave in 1959, 1976, and 1997. The rivalry engendered by the conclaves became so intense that by 1962 comments were made that "Georgia enrolls professionals the semester [*quarter actually*] before Conclave." Perhaps this was because the "Timber Dawgs" had won four out of the last five.[65]

The University of Georgia student chapter of the Wildlife Society was founded in 1967. It has consistently placed first or near the top in the Southern Wildlife Quiz Bowl competition.

A 1950 research report by the School of Forestry noted significant advances had been made in regenerating and protecting the forest. It cited particular success in

statewide fire protection and seedling production for small landowners.[66] The report set out an ambitious research agenda with a strong case for state funding in ten broad areas ranging from stand establishment to harvesting, watershed management to marketing, and economics to wildlife management. Twenty subgroups of specific research budgets were presented.[67]

After the Georgia Forest Research Council was placed under control of GFC, the School had an immediate need to secure a steady funding source.[68] It issued a detailed ten-year research plan that proposed looking at many of the areas mentioned in the 1950 report. However, there were some additions including more emphasis on biotechnology, recreation and the economic, social, legal, and financial aspects of resource management.

In 1979 the state's forest cover was 25.2 million acres or 67 percent of the total state land area.[69] The total economic contribution for forestry was $4.2 billion.[70]

Top: Sophomore summer camp at Hard Labor Creek State Park, 1956. *Courtesy WSFNR*

Bottom: Dean Al Herrick and Miss Lumberjack, ca. early 1960s. *Courtesy GFC*

Where Are We Headed In Wildlife Management?

By James H. Jenkins

"The Southeast is potentially the greatest deer producing area in North America." How well I remember this statement made by Dr. Ira N. Gabrielson a scant eight years ago. Dr. Gabrielson is the president of the Wildlife Management Institute, a privately supported conservation organization, and was formerly director of the U. S. Fish and Wildlife Service during an era which saw the comeback of our North American waterfowl. Yet several of the Northern states harvest ten times the number of deer that are taken in most of the Southeastern states. On the other hand most of the wild turkeys of the U. S. are in the Southeast although they originally ranged over most of eastern North America.

John H. Henderson, Jr., veterinary student, and Johnny L. Jernigan helping Drs. Jenkins and Hayes on cooperative deer capturing project with

Ca. 1950s. *Courtesy WSFNR*

Preparing Professionals

Research cooperation between the School and the U.S. Forest Service started in 1939. Through the political power of Georgia U.S. Senator Dick Russell, the Forest Service received several large appropriations beginning in 1954 for research and facilities in Athens.[71] The long cooperation between the two groups enabled each to concentrate on problems without direct competition. This enabled the School to develop a strong graduate program that helped train Forest Service scientists. And it developed "…a partnership unique in forestry research and education which has served as a model for other institutions in this country and abroad."[72]

In 1980 Leon "Buddy" Hargreaves, former Forestry Club president and professor of the School of Forest Resources, was appointed dean following Dean Herrick's retirement. Hargreaves oversaw significant increases in the School's endowment during the UGA Bicentennial Capital Campaign with the able assistance of Professor Hank Haynes. Buddy was a tough administrator, and he labored for many years to secure funding for Forestry Building Four and the L. L. "Pete" Phillips Wood

Products Utilization and Plant Sciences Building. He was rebuffed either by the university, Board of Regents, or General Assembly on numerous occasions for various reasons—some budgetary and some political. He recruited the assistance of the Georgia Forestry Association and the Jayhole Club, and funding was found on the last day of the 1989 General Assembly session.

The School significantly expanded its programs in wildlife management, fisheries, and aquaculture and biotechnology while it continued its strong orientation to quantitative timber management. The Hargreaves-led faculty studied but never implemented a five-year professional curriculum.[73] Hargreaves' administration also marked a changing of the guard as the WWII generation faculty retired. Aggressive new faculty members were recruited in expanding disciplines.

Hargreaves had a strong business management background and, in the early 1980s, he recruited Professors Hank Haynes, Russ Milliken, and Tom Harris, Jr., from the private sector to establish the Center for Forest Business Management.[74, 75] The renamed Center for Forest Business was officially approved by the Board of Regents in September 1997, and Bob Izlar was recruited to become the first director.

Professor Andy Campbell provided a good perspective on what the School's increased prominence meant:

> *The revitalized School of Forest Resources enabled the University of Georgia to develop what is now nationally recognized as an area of competence in forestry equal to the best in the nation. By developing a strong forestry program, at a high educational and technical level, the University has been able to attract funding from federal and other sources and as a result its graduates and research.[76]*

Summer camp trip with Dr. Jack May, Santee River bottom, Francis Marion National Forest, 1963. *Courtesy WSFNR*

With his dream of financial security for the School realized and with Building Four under construction, Hargreaves retired in 1991. Arnett C. Mace, Jr., buried his ugly Florida orange and blue and became dean in 1991. He served until he was promoted to university senior vice president for academic affairs and provost in 2002. Mace oversaw the next highly successful phase of the capital endowment campaign, the dedication of the new building in 1993, construction of the Warnell Center in Effingham County, and the renaming of the School of Forest Resources. He obtained direct state funding for five new faculty positions and research support for forest sustainability studies.

The School's name evolved from the George Foster Peabody School of Forestry, in concept; to Department of Forestry; to Division of Forestry; to George Foster Peabody School of Forestry; to School of Forest Resources; and finally to the Daniel Brooks Warnell School of Forest Resources in 1991. The School was renamed and dedicated to Daniel Brooks Warnell on April 12, 1991. As a legislator, Warnell was a strong supporter of Herty's research work on improved turpentine processes and developing the southern pulp and paper industry. "Mr. Danny" saw Georgians could recover from adversity "...to build a future through the wise use and faithful stewardship of that land resource

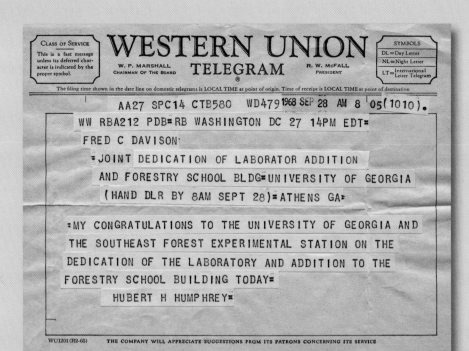

WESTERN UNION TELEGRAM

CLASS OF SERVICE
This is a fast message unless its deferred character is indicated by the proper symbol.

W. P. MARSHALL
CHAIRMAN OF THE BOARD

R. W. McFALL
PRESIDENT

SYMBOLS
DL=Day Letter
NL=Night Letter
LT=International Letter Telegram

The filing time shown in the date line on domestic telegrams is LOCAL TIME at point of origin. Time of receipt is LOCAL TIME at point of destination

AA27 SPC14 CTB580   WD479 1968 SEP 28 AM 8 05(1010).

WW RBA212 PDB=RB WASHINGTON DC 27 14PM EDT=

FRED C DAVISON·

=JOINT DEDICATION OF LABORATOR ADDITION

AND FORESTRY SCHOOL BLDG=UNIVERSITY OF GEORGIA

(HAND DLR BY 8AM SEPT 28)=ATHENS GA=

=MY CONGRATULATIONS TO THE UNIVERSITY OF GEORGIA AND

THE SOUTHEAST FOREST EXPERIMENTAL STATION ON THE

DEDICATION OF THE LABORATORY AND ADDITION TO THE

FORESTRY SCHOOL BUILDING TODAY=

HUBERT H HUMPHREY=

WU1201 (R2-65)   THE COMPANY WILL APPRECIATE SUGGESTIONS FROM ITS PATRONS CONCERNING ITS SERVICE

Top: 1968 congratulatory telegram from U.S. Vice President Hubert Humphrey. *Courtesy WSFNR*

Bottom: New School of Forestry and Natural Resources complex, northern view, 1968. *Courtesy WSFNR*

Arkansas A&M and Mississippi State University before beginning a highly successful career in forest industry. He retired in 2002 as executive vice president of Champion International. Porterfield has brought his executive experience to bear in forging a new direction for the School while retaining roots in its areas of strength. Under his leadership, the School once more changed its name to better reflect its expanding mission of teaching, research and outreach. It became the Daniel Brooks Warnell School of Forestry and Natural Resources on February 21 in its Centennial Year.

The School's reputation was strongly formed in the 1950s, and it continues to be widely admired and respected. Both the Seaboard Airline Railroad and the Georgia Forestry Commission issued special publications to celebrate the School's golden anniversary in 1956.[78, 79] The GFC editorial noted the finest tribute to the School of Forestry was its graduates and the good they had done:[80]

> *Only the past is certain; the future has a habit of never quite turning out as we would expect. One fact is certain, the School of Forest Resources has for 100 years faithfully served the forestry profession of Georgia and the Nation. The School has fulfilled the hope expressed by Alfred Gaskin of the U.S. Forest Service when he spoke at the Division of Forestry inauguration on that November night a century ago: "I sincerely hope that the establishment of a Forestry School in Georgia means more than an opportunity for young men to become professional foresters. There should flow from this institution an influence for the proper understanding of the objects of forestry that shall be felt all over the State." The challenge now is to continue this "proper understanding" of forest resources into an always uncertain future.*[81]

and hard work."[77] Under the leadership of graduate student Demetrius "Deek" Cox, Xi Chapter of Xi Sigma Pi designed and funded the beautiful lobby bench in front of the D. B. Warnell portrait in 2001.

Interim Dean Dr. James Sweeney succeeded Mace and served until 2004. Dr. Richard Porterfield was selected as permanent dean and took office January 1, 2004. Porterfield had a strong academic background at

Bob Grogan (class of 1931), the School's oldest living alumnus as of 2005, 1980. *Courtesy Bob Grogan*

School of Forestry and Natural Resources recruitment brochure, 1968. *Courtesy WSFNR*

Left: Forestry students in longleaf-wiregrass, 2000. *Courtesy WSFNR*

Below: Dr. Sarah Covert preparing lab sample, 2000. *Courtesy WSFNR*

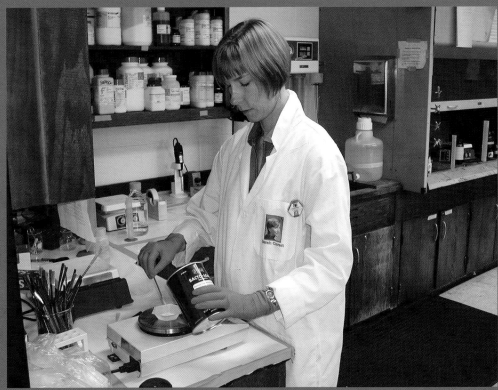

Top: Eminent Scholar Dr. Bruce Beck sampling water quality, 2000. *Courtesy WSFNR*

Bottom: Mary Anne McGuire measuring stem respiration in Biosphere 2, 2003. *Courtesy WSFNR*

Guoyuan Li sampling water, 2005. *Courtesy WSFNR*

Opposite page: Erin Moore learning to use GPS, ca. early 2000s. *Courtesy WSFNR*

3
A Need for Advocacy

Stirring Interest

Peabody made his gift to fund the Forest School to specifically benefit rural Georgians.[1] Chancellor Barrow was successful in recruiting a native Georgian, Georgia graduate and experienced forester when he got Professor Akerman. Barrow's close friend, Tom Reed, said the interest of the state needed to be stirred up, and "Professor Akerman lost no time in stirring up interest....He called a meeting of Georgia citizens interested in forestry which was held in Athens on March 1, 1907, at which time the Georgia Forestry Association was organized."[2,3] In his 1907 annual report, Akerman reported, "I am also acting temporarily as the Secretary and Treasurer of the Georgia Forestry Association, an organization which has for its object the promotion of the art and science of forestry in this state."[4]

Leon Brown recounted the Association's early days:

> According to the brochure published by the group, they were "organized to promote the conservation and perpetuation of the timber resources of Georgia, to advocate the passage and enforcement of proper forest fire laws and to assist in arousing a healthy public sentiment in regard to our forests."

Opposite page: Chuck Leavell, 1999 National Tree Farmer of the Year, as Project Learning Tree instructor. *Courtesy GFA*

The first order of business for this new organization was the publication of a magazine, "Southern Woodlands—a Journal of Forestry, Lumbering, Wood Manufacture and Related Sciences and Industries." In the first issue of that magazine, there was a statement of purpose along with a status report on the Forest Reserve Bill pending in Congress. Even though there were several interesting editions of the magazine, the organized efforts of the Georgia Forest [sic] Association failed due to lack of financial support.[5]

In an undated pamphlet published by Akerman as secretary of the Georgia Forestry Association, he said, "Forest Association should be changed to a reading club for literature coming from the 'Forest School'" because of declining dues and increasing expenses. Brown continued the story:

Soon after the GFA demise, the cause of forestry from the private sector was represented by the Georgia Forestry Committee of the Southern Forestry Congress. On January 30, 1921 at a Committee meeting in Atlanta, the following resolution was passed: "Resolved that this committee as organized also functions as the Georgia Forestry Association until such time as the Executive Committee of this organization sees fit to call a state convention to elect officers, adopt a constitution and bylaws and other details for a permanent and distinctive organization." Thus the birth of the modern Georgia Forestry Association.

The first objectives of the fledgling Association was to start a campaign of education to convince the state legislature of the need to protect Georgia forests through the establishment of a state forestry department. After four years of intense lobbying, the General Assembly passed a bill creating the Georgia Forestry Department on August 14, 1925.

After this number one goal had been accomplished, the GFA settled into the position of acting in an advisory capacity to the newly created Department. The Association sponsored fire control measures across the state, along with legislation to create and finance the Herty Pulp and Paper Laboratory at Savannah.[6]

The Georgia Forestry Association

EXTENDS congratulations to the graduating class of the School of Forestry and our best wishes for a successful year.

We say to the undergraduates: Take advantage of your opportunity and finish the course.

The Georgia Forestry Association, organized in 1921, is a volunteer organization for the promotion of education in forestry and the best practices in the propagation, care and utilization of our forests, with which Georgia is so richly endowed.

T. G. WOOLFORD,
President,
Atlanta, Georgia

ALEX. CASSELS,
Secretary,
Savannah, Georgia

Top: Early GFA promotional card, ca. 1930s. *Courtesy WSFNR*

Middle: A good firefighting technique if the horse doesn't spook, ca. 1920s. *Courtesy WSFNR*

Bottom: Early loggers found easy pickings, as typified by this large hardwood, ca. 1920s. *Courtesy WSFNR*

But the stage was not completely set. There were reasons to stir things up. How do you encourage people to want to change their practices? What about wildfire? Prior to the enactment of the 1921 Forestry Board law, the only laws regarding forestry were related to an 1833 law[7] regarding arson and an 1856 law[8] dealing with fire liability of railroad companies. The American Tree Association reported that railroads were liable for fires they caused, but "lack of funds makes forest protection system impossible."[9]

Hated taxes were another concern. Even in 1900, Bruncken noted, "No species of property is hit more hardly by the crudities of the tax laws than timberland."[10] Many years later, William Duerr found the same problem: "The general property tax has long been regarded as a major, and at times as even an insuperable, obstacle to the practice of sustained-yield forestry by private owners."[11]

Besides fire, pigs, the destructive turpentine "box" technique, and taxes, landowners had other concerns. What should they do? What could they do? What markets were there? How would they pay for it? Who could help them? One of these problems alone at the time was a conundrum, but all of these?[12, 13]

At the beginning of the twentieth century, there were several forest products associations operating in various southern states as well as southwide.[14] The Georgia Sawmill Association, founded in 1889, became the Georgia Interstate Sawmill Association in 1903. In 1906 it evolved into the Georgia-Florida Sawmill Association and operated as such until merging with the Southern Forest Products Association in 1926.[15] At its height, it had more than 150 member mills and represented about 700 million board feet of production.

The American Turpentine Farmers Association Cooperative was founded in Valdosta in 1934. Judge Harley Langdale, Sr., was one of the founding members. It continues to represent the industry today.[16, 17, 18] Langdale closed their last turpentine still August 16, 1975, and for all practical reasons, that was the end of the turpentine industry. At one time they had twenty-five stills made of copper.[19] GFA encouraged the use of the cup-and-gutter system perfected by Herty.[20]

Top: Loading pulpwood onto barges on the Savannah River for towing to Savannah to be made into paper, 1937. Each barge holds about 150 cords of pulp. (Sutherlands Bluff, McIntosh County). *Courtesy Ted Walker/USFS*

Bottom: Typical Georgia turpentine still, ca. 1910s. *Courtesy Ted Walker/USFS*

Harley Langdale recounted his early problems getting people interested in reforestation. Banks would not loan money on timberland or sawmills unless the owners had other assets. The saying was, "If he has sawdust in the cuffs of his pants, don't loan him any money." The only way a sawmiller could get money was to go through a factor, and they charged anywhere from 8 percent to 20 percent commission and often got a part of your business. Langdale saw this as a serious impediment

Top left: "Pecker wood" portable sawmill, ca. 1940s. *Courtesy TLC*

Top right: "High lead" loading logs, ca. 1940s. *Courtesy TLC*

Middle: Special forestry days for public relations included parades and themed floats. Forest Festival Parade, Valdosta, Georgia, 1947. *Courtesy TLC*

Bottom: Shortwood rail car arriving at Rayonier's Jesup, Georgia, mill, 1954. *Courtesy Rayonier*

to developing a vibrant forest products industry, so he lobbied along with others to get banking laws changed so the new saying would be, "That man has sawdust in his pants cuffs and we like to see him coming." Still, Langdale remembers it was hard for even him to borrow money through normal financial channels, so he borrowed money from Rayonier and paid them back in pulpwood. This made banks start to realize there was value in timberland and forestry.[21, 22]

In the beginning of Langdale's career, foresters did not know what pulpwood was. Turpentine people did not want to see pulpwood mills come because they thought those mills would cut all the timber. When Langdale was in forestry school in the 1930s, turpentine was the most important woods crop. Then, poles became an important crop. During the same time, the cypress market was enhanced by the demise of the chestnut.[23]

In 1944 the Federal Crop Insurance program was authorized to insure timber and forests, but there was no move to do so. Federally chartered national banks were prohibited from making loans secured by forest land until 1953.[24]

As acting head of the UGA Division of Forestry, DuPre Barrett lamented the 1930 condition of Georgia's forests:

Destructive lumbering followed by forest fires has left many millions of acres in Georgia idle, for there were left no seed trees to restock the land in man's eagerness to remove

Hand planting with a dibble, ca. 1950s. *Courtesy TLC*

EXECUTIVE DEPARTMENT
ATLANTA

Herman E. Talmadge   William H. Kimbrough
Governor   Executive Secretary

GEORGIA FORESTRY DAY

A PROCLAMATION

WHEREAS: The forests of Georgia constitute one of the State's most important natural resources; and

WHEREAS: The conservation of this natural resource is of paramount importance to the welfare of the State and of the Nation; and

WHEREAS: The School of Forestry of the University of Georgia, through its graduates, is contributing to the proper protection, development and use of our forests; and

WHEREAS: The students, alumni and friends of the School of Forestry are joining in the celebration of a Forestry Day with appropriate ceremonies;

NOW, THEREFORE, I Herman E. Talmadge, Governor of the State of Georgia, do hereby proclaim Saturday, May 5, 1951, as Forestry Day throughout the State. and do further recommend to the people of this State that they protect our forests from fire and waste and that they give earnest consideration to the replenishing of this renewable resource, to the end that the future benefits from this resource be greatly enhanced.

IN WITNESS WHEREOF, I have hereunto set my hand and caused to be affixed the Executive Seal of Georgia at the Capitol in Atlanta, Georgia, this 7th day of February, Nineteen Hundred and Fifty-one.

s/t/ Herman E. Talmadge
GOVERNOR

BY THE GOVERNOR:
s/t/ William H. Kimbrough
SECRETARY, EXECUTIVE DEPARTMENT

Forestry Day Executive Proclamation of Governor Herman Talmadge, 1951. *Courtesy WSFNR*

all value from the land. . . . Land that once grew forests can always grow forests, produce revenue, pay taxes and give employment, if properly managed. If land is handled with no thought of future production and remains idle land, other land must pay for such idleness. One reason why there is so much idle land is that the owners do not know how to use these acres with the assurance that profitable returns will reward their enterprise. In cutting away our forests we have harvested a crop we did not sow. This has sustained a large industry for many years in Georgia but the end to this opportunity is drawing near.[25]

Rebirth and Progress

GFA Secretary Bonnell H. Stone picked up on GFA's development in relation to those problems and times:

Hand loading shortwood pulpwood. Notice pulpwood pens, ca. 1950s. *Courtesy Sam Killian*

Newly produced paper at Rayonier's Jesup, Georgia, mill, 1954. *Courtesy Rayonier*

This association became inactive as a result of a letter vote taken by the secretary, and the seal, by-laws, etc., are now in possession of the writer, having been presented to our present Georgia Forestry Association after its organization was perfected in Macon in June, 1922.

One result of the Third Southern Forestry Congress held in Atlanta, was a resolution requesting the Georgia Committee to remain active and increase the membership of same through appointment by the Chairman. Close cooperation was established between this "Georgia Forestry Committee" and the Georgia State Board of Forestry, and when Governor Hardwick organized this Board (and under the law became the first President of same), he invited the members of the Committee to sit in at the meeting in his office and offer such suggestions as they saw fit.

Since the Board had no funds for its investigative work, the Committee offered its services which were gladly accepted by the Board, and this spirit of cooperation has brought about some important results and continues to exist for placing forestry on its own merits through this distinctive movement in Georgia.

Prior to the State Forestry Convention held in June, 1922, under the auspices of the Georgia Forestry Committee, The American Forestry Association assigned its Forester to special work in

the headquarters office of this Committee without expense to us. This resulted in the organization of The Georgia Forestry Association as a permanent and independent body.[26]

The 1933 by-laws and constitution laid out four specific purposes for GFA. These were to secure legislative passage of adequate forest policy, encourage forestry practice by private landowners, stimulate public interest in forestry, and to cooperate with similar associations.[27] These were the amended Articles of Association originally adopted June 7, 1922.

Leon Brown explained GFA's activities after the 1922 reorganization.

The late Twenties and early Thirties saw the GFA become dedicated to the establishment and financing of the George Foster Peabody School of Forestry at the

University of Georgia. The goal of promoting quality forestry education was to become the longest sustained project of the GFA, and remains today as one of the Association's primary and most important functions.

The Thirties were tumultuous years for the entire country. It was no different for forestry. The GFA set about the task of addressing and solving the most serious threat to the industry to date – Fire. Many people today tend to forget how serious this problem once was. But as T. G. Woolford, past president of the Association, said in an interview in 1938, "Fire and the lack of fire protection is the biggest problem we have in Georgia forestry. In one day a fire can do more damage than nature can repair in 100 years."

It seems that the forest fire problem was twofold. First, very few Georgians had any respect for the woodlands, and second, there was no organization or official body to fight fires once they started. The Association combated the first problem by mounting a massive media campaign aimed at educating the public as to the value of Georgia woodlands. The Association pushed heavily for legislation that would tighten woods arson laws in order to discourage the indiscriminate setting of fires.

But the problem of fighting fires was very difficult since no one knew who should take the responsibility. Again, the GFA took the initiative by pushing for a constitutional amendment that would allow counties to spend local funds to fight forest fires. As Woolford said, "No city would consider for a moment being without a fire department. Yet I am sure forest fires do more damage in the state every year than do fires in our cities." The amendment passed by a margin of four to one due partly because of the intense campaigning by members of the GFA.[28]

Legislative Success

Buddy Hargreaves' Ph.D. dissertation at the University of Michigan is an excellent administrative study of a state agency, in this case the Georgia Forestry Commission. He gave a very thorough review of the Commission's founding and early years. A General Assembly bill was passed in 1921 to create a State Board of Forestry to survey forest conditions. A Board was appointed, and it sought to get a law passed giving statutory authority to the Board, but the bill failed. This caused GFA, which was reorganized in 1922, to concentrate its efforts on creating a separate forestry agency in state government. GFA was successful this time, and the General Assembly passed a bill in August 1925 creating the State Board of Forestry "…consisting of the Governor, Secretary of State, State Geologist, Director of Agricultural Extension, and five citizens of the state. The five citizens were to be appointed by the Governor, one to represent women's civic organizations and four to represent lumbering, lumber manufacturing, farming, and naval stores or timber owning interests in the state. They were to be named with reference to geographical location within the state."[29]

Top: Testing experimental radios for firefighting, 1955. Curtis Barnes, GFC. *Courtesy WSFNR*

Bottom: GFA-GFRC public relations campaign for scientific forestry, ca. 1950s. *Courtesy WSFNR*

Top left: A crop of boxes. Later stages of the naval stores industry with tin cup-and-gutter system, ca. 1950s. *Courtesy Sam Killian*

Top right: Eley C. Frazer III scaling a cypress log for St. Joe Paper Company in 1957. *Courtesy F&W Forestry Services, Inc.*

Bottom: A weak method of fighting wildfire, ca. 1950s. *Courtesy Sam Killian*

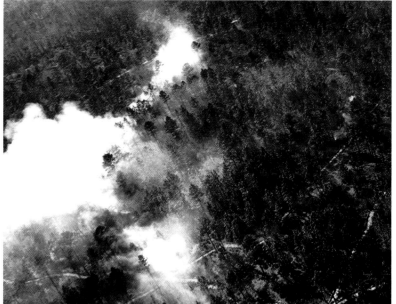

In 1936 H. H. Chapman, in his role as president of the Society of American Foresters, wrote Governor Talmadge questioning the professional qualifications of Dyal, who was recently appointed as Georgia state forester. He noted the statutory requirement of a "technically trained forester with at least two year's experience in technical and administrative work." He went on to write, "We find Mr. Dyal is not in any sense of the word technically trained and that he has never had an hour's technical instruction in any school or department of forestry."[34] In the letter, he noted there was a "State Forest School" in Athens and that it had been there since 1906 and graduated seventy-one foresters.

Talmadge tersely responded, "He [Dyal] is a born forester. A wood ranger right. He was born down in the Okefenokee Swamp."[35] Chapman's response was equally terse in noting Dyal was not a born forester and that if the state wanted him as state forester, then it should

In 1926 a state appropriation of $13,402.42 and a federal grant of $4,185.15 helped the Board get started. Timber protective organizations were set up beginning in 1927. Governor Russell reorganized state government in 1931 and drastically reduced state departments from 117 to 17. The State Forestry Board was absorbed into the State Department of Forestry and Geological Development. Power to appoint the state forester was transferred to the governor.

The General Assembly appropriated $20,000 for "the operation and maintenance of an experimental pulp and paper laboratory." After securing additional funding, the laboratory began research in 1932 under the direction of Dr. Charles H. Herty.[30, 31, 32]

In 1937 state government was reorganized yet again, and the State Forestry Board was moved into the newly created Department of Natural Resources. The law authorizing this also specified that the director of the new Division of Forestry must be a graduate of the University of Georgia School of Forestry or a recognized forestry program. This was in response to a State Forest Board rule of qualifications of the state forester that was ignored by Governor Eugene Talmadge when he appointed Elmer Dyal as state forester in 1936.[33]

Top: TVA Forester Ben Cobb at Dade County, Georgia, forestry meeting, ca. 1950s. *Courtesy Ted Walker/USFS*

Bottom: A "bicycle" chain saw surely beat a "gator tail" crosscut, ca. 1950s. *Courtesy Ted Walker/USFS*

repeal the law and close the School. This letter mentions that the School graduated not seventy-one but seventy-two foresters.[36]

A constitutional amendment in 1939 authorized counties to levy taxes for natural resource conservation and forest protection. The Division was able to leverage these funds into county-wide fire protection units and federal assistance in wildfire protection.[37]

The Department of Natural Resources was abolished in 1943, and the Division became the Department of Forestry under a new Division of Conservation. As one might deduce from this seemingly constant reorganization and shifting authority, the state forester's job was a political one. The unusual step was taken in this reorganization to prescribe a full hearing before the governor and the deans of the University of Georgia School of Forestry and Georgia Tech before a state forester could be removed from office.[38] Another law passed in 1943 made woods arson a felony.[39]

The present Georgia Forestry Commission was created in January 1949 and officially replaced the Georgia Department of Forestry July 1, 1949. According to Hargreaves, "This act was the result of concerted efforts by persons interested in forestry to remove the appointment of the State Forester from the Governor's office. From 1936 to 1948, eight men had served the state in the capacity of head of the forestry agency. Leaders in forestry felt

there was a great need for a more stable administration of the forestry agency." The new law specified that the director of the Forestry Commission would be appointed by the commissioners who were appointed by the governor.[40]

When it came to Gene Talmadge's son, forestry had a better friend in the governor's office. Herman Talmadge was one of Georgia's most "woods savvy" governors and a lifelong supporter of forestry. He stated, "Getting into timber was one of the smartest decisions I've ever made."[41] "Uncle Hummon" was a friend of forestry from his time as governor through his U.S. Senate days when he was chairman of the Senate Agriculture, Forestry and Nutrition Committee.

When Talmadge took office as governor, he saw an idling economic engine in forestry. But "without adequate fire protection and clear-sighted political leadership, the economic potential of our forests is going to waste."[42] He wrote about the fire conditions at the time when you could not drive on the roads because thick smoke from wildfires made the roads impassable. He felt certain that money spent on fire protection and forestry would encourage an economic boon, and he noted, "Those benefits have exceeded our wildest expectations....But the true measure of what we did does not lie in the amount of money spent or the number of programs started. Instead, one must look at the progress made by forest industries in Georgia during the time I was in office and in the years since to see what a dividend we have reaped from our investment in forestry."[43]

Top: Marking a witness tree used to find surveyed property corners, ca. 1950s. *Courtesy Sam Killian*

Bottom: Closeup of wheel saw bucking swamp blackgum, Sapelo Forest, ca. 1956–57. *Courtesy IP*

To see how far the state advanced under the revitalized GFA and GFC, it is helpful to see what the first official report said about the state of the forests. In 1926 the State Forestry Department released its first report to the governor and General Assembly. This first report gives a clear snapshot

Top left: Typical multipass site preparation with rolling drum chopper, ca. 1950s. *Courtesy Sam Killian*

Top right: Early helicopter used in direct seeding and aerial fire detection work, ca. 1950s. *Courtesy Sam Killian*

Bottom: Early industrial pine pulpwood plantation, ca. 1950s. *Courtesy Sam Killian*

Typical radio command post used in firefighting in the 1950s. *Courtesy Sam Killian*

of the state of Georgia's forest. The state had 23.9 million acres of timberland representing 63.7 percent of the total land area. Any land capable of producing a greater profit from forestry than that of row crops was defined as "forest land."[44] Six million of these acres were considered idle or unproductive. There were less than 1 million acres of virgin forest in 1926.[45]

The 1925 production of 1,130 sawmills was 1.3 billion board feet with a stumpage value of $6.7 million and a finished value of $27.1 million. The very clear point was made that if the state's forests were properly managed, the increased value in production and stumpage would be an astounding $140 million.

In 1925 there were sixty-five counties producing naval stores from 6,185 crops (a crop is 10,000 trees) by 581 operators employing 12,458 people. The economic value to the state was an additional $23 million in 1926.[46] Georgia's peak lumber production was more than 1.3 billion board feet in 1909. That dropped off to 761 million feet in 1920 and rebounded to 1.2 billion feet in 1921.[47]

Fourteen timber protective organizations (TPO's) covering 1.3 million acres were set up with members paying 2.5 to 3 cents per acre per year to employ fire patrolmen. A TPO represented any organized landowner group representing 10,000 acres or more.[48]

The Forestry Department actively provided management advice to private landowners and charged only for travel expenses.[49] Even in 1926, there was the keen recognition that forestry education in primary and secondary schools was vitally important to long-term conservation success:

> *A plan of introducing forestry studies in the public schools without overloading the present curricula with new text books is being worked out cooperatively with the State Superintendent of Schools. The complete project will correlate forestry with lessons in history, English, arithmetic, etc. ...*[50]

The State Forestry Department instituted a prize essay contest conducted by the Georgia Forestry Association. Some 5,000 "forestry primers" were developed and distributed to teachers for the contest.[51]

Growing Georgia

As progress was being made in reforestation, with Herty's discoveries at the Savannah laboratory on the feasibility of making newsprint and kraft paper from highly resinous, Deep South pines, and with GFA's political leadership, the forest economy of Georgia started to brighten considerably. Northern manufacturers started to take note of the Southern Phoenix. This is well illustrated by Union Camp's former CEO, Craig McClelland. The skepticism of northern mills toward moving south to tap into Herty's discovery was typified by the situation of Union Bag in 1934. Union Bag President Sandy Calder and his brother snapped up stock at $5.50 a share. McClelland said, "In a year, they controlled the company and told the directors— northern roots be damned—they were heading South." The first Union Bag paper machine started in 1936 in Savannah. By 1938 the company had three machines rolling out paper and a bag plant on the Savannah

Kirk Sutlive receiving public relations award at UGA banquet, 1957. *Courtesy WSFNR*

Railroad shortwood yard, which could be found throughout the South before the Staggers Rail Deregulation Act of 1980, ca. 1950s. *Courtesy Sam Killian*

River.[52] This site eventually became home to the largest pulp and paper mill in the world.

Union Bag and Paper Corporation [later Union Camp] began its long support of GFA at an Athens meeting in 1937. "It would adopt a constructive forest policy to perpetuate its pulpwood supply and would inaugurate a program that would insure [*sic*] permanent forestry operations on both company lands and other privately owned lands."[53] This was a bold policy for the time.

As GFA came through WWII, its finances had stabilized, and it began to take up its advocacy role with the general public as described below by Leon Brown:

> By the late 1940's the Association had turned the heads of enough important people to really get support for the anti-forest fire campaign. The GFA accepted the responsibility of sponsoring the "Keep Green" program for Georgia. The purpose of the "Keep Georgia Green" movement was to bring to the attention of every Georgian through mass education the important fact that the destruction of trees by fire not only deprives the owner of income and users of a source of raw material, but also affects the well-being of every person within the boundaries of the state.

> The "Keep Georgia Green" movement was one of the most intensive campaigns ever launched by an independent Association. Every media vehicle available was incorporated into the movement. Civic clubs and service organizations were recruited to tell the forest and forest fire story. Signs saying "Keep Georgia Forests Green" were made available to every county in the state. In 1951 the Association launched a "Keep Georgia Forests Green" county contest. This was an entirely new approach to the forest fire problem and continued until recently.

> Besides fire, the "Keep Georgia Green" movement also incorporated emphasis on tree planting and regeneration. By the end of the 1960s, "Keep Georgia Green" had become a familiar slogan in the lives of all Georgians.

> One of the aims of the GFA has always been to support sound forestry practices that will perpetuate a continuing forest resource in Georgia. For this reason, it was only natural that the Association would join with the Georgia Forestry Commission and the Southern Pine Association and become one of the sponsors of the Tree Farm System in Georgia.[54]

Mead Corporation was another northern company that came to Georgia early but in a tentative way. Its Georgia operations were always joint ventures.

In 1936 Mead entered a 50-50 arrangement with Scott Paper to build a pulpmill in Brunswick known as Brunswick Pulp and Paper.[55] Mead and Inland Container Corporation incorporated Macon Kraft in 1946 for purposes of a pulpmill in Macon.[56] The Mead-Inland Rome mill plans were drawn up in 1951, and the mill was producing in 1954.[57]

At the end of WWII, there were renewed calls for forest restoration. While the South had 44 percent of its land in forests, the goal was at least 60 percent. Richard Boerker noted, "…vast areas now in farms are too poor to afford a decent living. Such lands should be

retired from agricultural use and should be planted to forest crops."[58]

The first tree farm was certified in Georgia in 1948. The 200-acre farm was in Atkinson County and belonged to Mr. E. C. Fancher. Georgia's first National Tree Farmer of the Year was Milton N. "Buddy" Hopkins, Jr., of Osierfield. He wrote a delightful tale of his days on the land called *In One Place: The Natural History of a Georgia Farmer.*[59]

From the 1950s on, the combined hard work of GFA, GFC, and the School started to pay huge dividends for the state. Forest cover by 1950 had increased to 25 million acres, but less than 10 percent of the original forest remained. Georgia led the nation in naval stores production and was sixth nationally in lumber production. While pulp tonnage production was respectable, it had not begun to approach what it would become.[60]

While reforestation had begun as early as 1915,[61] the real turnaround was much later. A dramatic series of events led to an increase in forests. The first of these was the boll weevil attack in the 1920s, next the Great Depression, then rural population decline during WWII. These events caused a massive abandonment of farm land, which quickly reverted to forests. Finally, the Soil Bank program of the 1950s caused even more crop land to be planted in pines.[62]

Noted UGA scientist Gene Odum, called the "Father of Ecology," stated, "Southern

Top: Early "V" blade used in site preparation, ca. 1950s. *Courtesy Sam Killian*

Bottom: Road building in gumbo, ca. 1950s. *Courtesy Sam Killian*

Top: Beauty contests promoted forestry awareness, 1964. *Courtesy TLC*

Bottom left: Early shortwood storage pile at a pulpmill, ca. 1950s. *Courtesy WSFNR*

Bottom right: GFA annual meeting awards, 1962. *Courtesy TLC*

During the early 1960s, Calvin Raley uses a Prentice Loader to load hardwood logs onto a self-contained loader-hauler for transport to Telley-Corbett Box Company. Note lack of safety equipment. *Courtesy Steve Crawford, Jr.*

states have made a remarkable recovery from decades of depression, and economic and cultural measures now approach those of the rest of the nation."[63] By the end of the 1950s, the South's "ancient red-hill badge of shame" was replaced by verdant tree cover, and the "Indian summer haze of perennial forest burnings" was no more.[64]

International Paper established its Southlands Experiment Forest near Bainbridge in 1957. It is the nation's oldest, continuously operating forest products firm research forest.[65] The idea behind Southlands was to make it a complete forestry research center to examine everything from tree genetics to fiber characteristics to soils to wildlife.[66]

Renowned forest policy expert Henry Clepper noted GFA was a leader in forestry legislation and the pro-

motion of the "…protection, management, utilization, and marketing…" of forestry.[67]

While only one out of 206 pages in the 1957 Georgia agriculture market report is devoted to forestry, the 1955 value of harvested timber was $1.2 billion, and crude pine gum production was valued at $16.4 million.[68]

Union Bag-Camp's Belleville, Georgia, nursery was sown the first time in March 1958 to produce 22,000 seedlings for the 1958–59 planting season. These trees were planted on 32,000 acres of company land by machine and hand planting.[69] Union Bag-Camp planted its 100 millionth seedling in February 1960.[70] This has been repeated by many firms involved in nursery production either for industrial lands or commercially.

In covering GFA's seventy-fifth anniversary, Leon Brown brought the final years to a close:

Top: Rosin yard with modern barrels, ca. 1960s. *Courtesy TLC*

Bottom: Milton (Buddy) Hopkins, National Tree Farmer of 1981, is flanked by Bobby Taylor, left, president of the Georgia Forestry Association, and Jack Gnann, chairman of the Georgia Tree Farm Committee, near Osierfield, 1982. *Courtesy GFA*

The Sixties and Seventies were the time of the greatest growth of the GFA. People were finally realizing the value of their timberland and felt the need to organize in order to protect this resource. Basically,

the purpose of the GFA has not changed since its inception in 1907. Obviously, it is to promote and encourage proper protection, management, utilization and marketing of the forest resources within the state of Georgia!

The means in which to fulfill the above have intensified recently. In 1966, TOPS magazine was first introduced as a communication tool of the GFA. The intent of TOPS was and is to inform members and other interested parties in layman's terms of the scope of Georgia forestry.[71]

The GFA 1967 Annual Meeting was a look back and forward. With an organization that was first concerned about fire protection, fence laws, and political interference in GFC, it was a time to reflect on how much had been accomplished.[72] Forest Service Smokey Bear artist Harry Rossoll told about his designs for GFA's logo and the Georgia Registered Forester logo as symbols.[73] Noted forestry leaders Ray Shirley, GFC; J. E. McCaffrey, International Paper; E. V. McSwiney, Georgia Kraft; and John Duncan, Jr., Southern Railway System; each spoke on a specific period in "Georgia Forestry's Changing Times" from 1907 to the distant future of 1997.[74, 75, 76, 77] The next year, V. J. Sutton gave a review of the "Keep Georgia Green" campaign.[78]

The forest industry log truck inspection program was first started by GFA in 1968. Rayonier was the first company to get on board and sponsor the program with the Georgia State Patrol.[79] In later years, GFA led another log truck safety campaign with the help of WSFNR Professors Joe McNeel, Dale Greene, and Ben Jackson. GFA's first arson prevention award was given in 1982. There are also awards for timber and equipment theft prevention.[80]

Georgia We Grow Trees

One of GFA's hallmarks has been its involvement in public relations to encourage public education about forestry matters. It has done this through the "Keep Georgia Green" campaign, Tree Farm, Project Learning Tree, landowner meetings, parades, and beauty contests. Judy Weston Hicks of Abbeville was the first GFA-sponsored Miss Georgia Forestry, in 1940. The Miss Georgia Forestry contest was conducted by GFA at its annual meetings until 1991 when Kecia Strickland was crowned. It was the culmination of many Georgia Forestry Commission sponsored county-level "Forestry Queen" pageants. The American Turpentine Farmers Association sponsored a "Miss Gum Spirits of Turpentine" contest among the young ladies from gum-producing counties at the GFA pageant. In 1991 GFA's Board felt a beauty queen pageant was no longer appropriate for the times. The Georgia Forestry Commission sponsored the pageant for several additional years before it became privately run.[81]

During the 1990s, GFA's legislative involvement was on two fronts. The first was more of a federal orientation with the national environmental focus on wetlands. Tom Harris, Jr., from the School of Forest Resources; John

Top: Homemade upgrades to big stick loader on tandem truck, ca. 1960s. *Courtesy TLC*

Bottom: Pulpwood scooper, ca. 1960s. *Courtesy TLC*

Godbee, Jr., from Union Camp; Frank Green from GFC; and Larry Walker from Procter and Gamble devoted their attention to wetlands issues though GFA's Wetlands and Environmental Committees. Their efforts led to two complete revisions of Georgia's Best Management Practices guidelines in the late 1980s and mid-1990s.

At the state level, Dr. Dale Greene of the School of Forest Resources led a multiyear effort to include log truck safety inspections under the Public Service Commission. This led to a change in the law that made log truck safety inspection mandatory and resulted in a safer log truck fleet. Greene worked with Drs. Joe McNeel and Ben Jackson, also with WSFNR, and Randy Starling of Procter and Gamble to conduct a series of "Skilled Driver" training courses over several years to ensure compliance with the new law. Jackson also led an effort to monitor the increasing complexity of local county ordinances governing logging activities.

A major effort, which consumed a sizeable amount of time and resources, was the arduous campaign to reform Georgia's ad valorem tax laws on agricultural and forest lands. This became known as the Amendment Three campaign (Amendment Three was the 1990 constitutional ballot question number).

"We have in our State today a hodge-podge, inconsistent, and uncoordinated system of taxation which, like 'Topsy,' just grew." This passage was quoted from the 1949 "Preliminary Report of the Tax Revision Committee of the State of Georgia", and it explained the property tax situation facing rural landowners from then to 1990.[82] The road to the 1990 general election passage of Amendment Three was a long one. It took twenty-four years of perseverance by GFA and the Georgia Farm Bureau Federation. The idea came before the General Assembly in 1966 as S.R. 15, but it failed by one vote. In the intervening years, various bills were introduced, but nothing happened. A partial solution was reached with the agricultural preferential treatment constitutional amendment in 1984. The rising tide of tax reform became so great that five separate bills were introduced in 1989. Then, the Georgia Department of Revenue, mistakenly interpreting a federal tax case, decided to direct each county to separate land from timber on the

Top: Two generations of Georgia pines, 2005. *Courtesy FIA*

Bottom left: Union Camp President Peter J. McLaughlin is assisted by nursery supervisor Paul Riggs (kneeling) as they plant the half-billionth tree on the company's Savannah Woodlands Region land, 1981. *Courtesy IP*

Bottom right: Union Bag Forester Tal Arnett demonstrates selective marking at 4-H Club Forestry Camp, ca. 1960s. *Courtesy Ted Walker/USFS*

Lifting seedlings at Union Camp's Bellville Nursery, Bellville, Georgia, ca. 1960s. *Courtesy IP*

digest and tax each. A meeting was held by Eley Frazer, Gene Robbins, and Bob Izlar with the Department of Revenue Property tax chief in August 1989 about the possibility of rescinding the new edict. The property tax chief said, "That is a policy question for the legislature. You'll have to take it up with them." They did.

The chairman of the House Ways and Means held four public hearings around the state. He got an earful and introduced House Resolution 836 in 1990. This measure passed and was placed on the ballot as constitutional amendment question number three.[83] The critical need for ad valorem tax reform proposed to be solved by Amendment Three was couched as being an environmental, urban, economic, tax, agricultural and financial issue for the voters.[84]

A campaign organization, the Coalition for a Green Georgia, was formed to raise money to promote Amendment Three's passage, and it enlisted the support of more than thirty conservation, forestry, environmental, citizen, and business groups.[85] Passage of Amendment Three was predicted to be revenue neutral.[86] National Tree Farmer of the Year C. M. Stripling wrote an impassioned article with four case studies illustrating the need for ad valorem tax reform for small forest and agricultural land owners. He noted that the situation had gotten so bad for him that if the amendment failed he would convert all his land assets to bonds.[87]

After an overwhelming voter approval of Amendment Three in urban, suburban and rural areas, GFA and its

Longwood and shortwood truck concentration yard, ca. early 1960s. *Courtesy Walter Jarck*

succeeding terms as chairs of GFA's Fiscal Policy Committee.

In 1990 GFA reached out to farm, wildlife, and environmental groups to form a legislative coalition for the passage of the Conservation Use Amendment. The coalition held together on several subsequent issues including the Mountain Protection Act, River Corridor Protection Act, and River Basin Management Act. In autumn 1994, GFA and the Georgia Farm Bureau Federation were approached by the Georgia Chapter of the Sierra Club following GFA's successful "We Grow Trees" Environmental Reunion to determine whether a common legislative agenda could be developed. From that invitation flowed an agreement by the three groups that later became known as the "unholy trinity" to develop a five-point forest and farmland protection action plan.[91]

One of the lessons learned in the Amendment Three campaign was that the forestry community needed a better public perception. This was not specific to Georgia; several national and state forestry associations had tried public relations campaigns of various types with equally varying success. After careful thought, the GFA Board selected a public relations campaign theme called Georgia We Grow Trees. GFA blitzed the state with "We Grow Trees" billboards, bumper stickers, license plates, apparel, and electronic and print media. The campaign rollout was hosted by U.S. Senator Sam Nunn in 1994 at the Atlanta Botanical Gardens. The appealing logo and strong message have been reaping benefits for Georgia forestry since then.

As part of its Georgia We Grow Trees public relations campaign, GFA hosted an Arbor Day world record-setting tree planting at Charlie Elliott Wildlife Center in Jasper County. Volunteers of all ages handily eclipsed the previous record of 5,500 trees by planting 14,000 loblolly pine seedlings in one day. Monticello Mayor Susan Holmes and Georgia DNR Commissioner Lonice

Judge Harley Langdale, Sr., with fully worked cat face, ca. late 1960s. *Courtesy TLC*

allies worked with the General Assembly to pass the very complicated enabling legislation.[88] After helping draft the enabling legislation, the GFA-led coalition then had to work with the Department of Revenue on issuing its regulations interpreting the enabling legislation to protect the interests of rural land taxpayers.[89, 90]

WSFNR professors Drs. John Gunter, Coleman Dangerfield, Jr., Fred Cubbage, and David Newman provided excellent guidance to GFA on federal and state tax matters. Gunter, Dangerfield, and Newman served

C. Barrett certified the tree planting record for the *Guinness Book of World Records*, and this record was later accepted and published.[92]

In cooperation with the Southeastern Wood Producers Association and American Forest and Paper Association, GFA began running the Georgia portion of the Sustainable Forestry Initiative® Program. This national program supports and enhances logger education, sustainable forestry practices and landowner outreach. The University of Georgia Center for Forest Business administers the logger education and landowner outreach portions of the SFI® Program under contract with GFA.

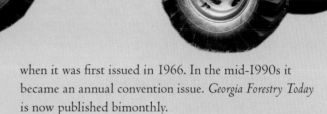

Early example of a shortwood forwarder, ca. early 1970s.
Courtesy Walter Jarck

In the early part of the twenty-first century, GFA actively worked on many fronts. Yet, it stuck to its core mission of providing advocacy for its members. In 2005 GFA was instrumental in helping create the General Assembly's Future of Forestry Study Committee, which held statewide meetings in its search for methods to enhance Georgia forestry's competitive position, focusing on the forest products industry and the funding needed to keep it healthy. Georgia Forestry Association also hosted the Governor's Summit on Forestry in September 2005 so state governmental and forestry leaders could develop a common, workable plan to maintain Georgia forestry's position as the economic and environmental driver of the state.

Through the years, GFA has used a publication system to communicate with its members and the public. Whether it was *Southern Woodlands*, *TOPS*, *GFA Legislative Bulletin*, or *GFA News*; the Association has always produced a quality publication. With the November/December 2005 issue of *Georgia Forestry Today*, GFA reached another milestone in publication excellence. *TOPS* was a quarterly magazine

when it was first issued in 1966. In the mid-1990s it became an annual convention issue. *Georgia Forestry Today* is now published bimonthly.

A dream of many GFA supporters was realized when the Georgia Forestry Foundation building was dedicated. It was planned many years ago, but the site and funding were always questionable. However, under the able leadership of Earl Smith and site supervision of David K. Mitchell, those dreams were beautifully fulfilled.

One hundred years have passed since Dean Akerman called that first meeting. One hundred years of progress in the direction of placing Georgia forestry in the position of prominence that it so richly deserves. From the one-man operation at the turn of the century to well-respected conservation leader, the Georgia Forestry Association was there, and will be there as forestry continues to grow Georgia.

Top: Allen-Jarck harvester, ca. early 1970s. *Courtesy Walter Jarck*

Bottom: Weyerhaeuser's Flint River pulpmill, Oglethorpe, Georgia (originally constructed by Buckeye Cellulose), 2005. *Courtesy Weyerhaeuser Company*

Jarck Go Getter, ca. early 1970s.
Courtesy Walter Jarck

Weyerhaeuser's Port Wentworth pulpmill, Port Wentworth, Georgia (originally constructed by Continental Can), 2005. *Courtesy Weyerhaeuser Company*

KEEP GEORGIA
VOTE YE

Paid for by the Coalition for a Green Georgia. Rudy Underwood, Chairman Bob Izlar

Top: Amendment Three campaign bumper sticker, 1990. *Courtesy Coalition for a Green Georgia*

Right: Typical hardwood sawmill layout in the 1970s. *Courtesy Georgia-Pacific*

Georgia's forestry leadership testifying before a 1989 U.S. Senate Committee hearing in Macon on restoration of timber capital gains tax treatment. (From left) B. Jack Warren, FLA executive vice president; John Mixon, GFC director; Bob Izlar, GFA executive director. *Courtesy FLA*

GREEN
S #3

Below: Governor Miller signing National Forest Products Week Proclamation, 1992. (L to R) Ed Cone, Arthur Howard, Mrs. Howard, Johnny Langdale, Mike Barnes, Governor Miller (seated), Fred Allen, John W. Mixon, Bob Izlar, Jack Warren, Walter Jarck. *Courtesy Office of the Governor*

Right: Blake Sullivan with Rosalynn and Jimmy Carter in a GFA Tree Farm PR still, 1991. *Courtesy GFA and AFF*

Below: Modern pine nursery, ca. 1990s. *Courtesy Rayonier*

Left: Laying down wood flakes in Oriented Strand Board production, 2000. *Courtesy TLC*

Below left: Evolution of GFA logo. *Courtesy GFA*

Below right: Lumber ready for kiln drying, 2000. *Courtesy TLC*

First seal used on copy of "Southern Woodlands" in 1907.

Logo designed by Smokey the Bear artist, Harry Rossoll, in 1939.

Similar to Rossoll's, late TOPS editor, Dexter Gatehouse, modified the letters GFA so they would be easier to distinguish.

Using a tree shaker to collect cones in a seed orchard, ca. 1980s. *Courtesy Sid Gray, Rayonier*

Top: Tree Farmer Vince Dooley giving keynote address at first State of the Forest Report release. (From left) Al Massey, Andy Stone, Dooley, Fred Allen, Jim Sweeney. School of Forest Resources, 2003. *Courtesy Frank M. Riley, Jr.*

Bottom: Dedication of Georgia Forestry Foundation Building, headquarters of GFA, May 13, 2004. *Courtesy GFA*

A Common Future 4

Both the School of Forestry and Natural Resources and Georgia Forestry Association started with grand aspirations. These dreams were then tempered through the years with disappointment, financial trouble, lack of direction, the Great Depression, two world wars, a "police action" in Korea, and a "conflict" in Vietnam, as well as indifferent political leadership. The School was started as a separate unit, put in the "dog house," reestablished as a stand-alone entity, almost closed, and rejuvenated. GFA started out much the same just four months after the School. After a period of initial interest and support, it floundered, was reorganized, had some spectacular success, went dormant, and was then revived.[1,2] Yet, during all these trials, there was always a core of dedicated people who made things happen. They had a passion about conservation, Georgia, and forestry specifically. For them, forestry was more than a vocation or avocation—it was a cause. A dedicated few can accomplish much. So it is with many organizations.

Here is an example. Harley Langdale, Jr., said, "I've seen my neighbors laugh when we would come in and plant a piece of land next to them in pines. They thought that this was foolish. But after a few years, when these trees would get up and be

Opposite page: UGA and GFA, a lasting partnership 1906–2006, 2003. *Courtesy Frank M. Riley, Jr.*

Savannah Pulp and Paper Laboratory, and promoting economic development through the pulp and paper and solid wood segments of the forest products industry. It is an enviable record of accomplishment that this book celebrates. The challenge for both organizations will be to stay out front and continue to lead. Markets for Georgia's market and non-market commodities must be well understood by the public and policy makers. Forest ecosystems produce literally hundreds of products, but the environmental products most Georgians take for granted—clean air and water, recreational opportunities, aesthetics, soil and water conservation, and wildlife—are demanded by the public with no compensation to the owners of these forests.

Doug MacCleery of the U.S. Forest Service has written an elegant little book on the resilience of the American forest. What he says in relation to them can apply equally to Georgia, if not more:

> *In recent years the growing urbanization, affluence, and mobility of Americans has caused a virtual revolution in the expectations and demands that the public places on forests. Some of these demands are in direct conflict with traditional forest values and uses.* [5] *"...the debate between people advocating the use and management of forests for commodity products and people wanting to minimize human influences and emphasize amenity values (particularly on public forests) has become increasingly shrill and divisive. On the positive side, it is a measure of the substantial success in past conservation policies that the United States now has the option to consider such choices.* [6] [Author's emphasis] *As human population increases and demands on natural resources grow, the challenge for society and its land managers is to find ways to realize both commodity products and amenity values from the same area of forest. This increasingly must become the dual focus for the concept of land stewardship and forest sustainability.* [7]

growing tall, we'd see them plow their land and plant pines also." [3] In writing about developing agriculture and forestry in the South, Robert Healy said we should strive to get better productivity on "...what may be the South's greatest natural resources, its nonindustrial private forests." [4]

The Warnell School of Forestry and Natural Resources and Georgia Forestry Association have been involved in the restoration and growth of Georgia forestry for a century. They have led in stopping destructive practices, educating professionals and the public, providing information to policy makers and landowners, establishing the Georgia Forestry Commission and the

If we do not, the last forest crop will be asphalt. [8]

Longleaf pine at Kinderlou in south Georgia, 2000. *Courtesy TLC*

Left: Old-time turpentine still preserved for demonstration and education, 2000. *Courtesy TLC*

Right: School of Forestry and Natural Resources PR logo, 2004. *Courtesy WSFNR*

Tall timber, 2005. Courtesy FIA

Left: Participants in Governor's Summit on Forestry convened by Governor Sonny Perdue, September 28, 2005.
Courtesy GFA

Below: WSFNR complex, 2004.
Courtesy WSFNR

Champions of Forestry

appendix one

George Foster Peabody
1852–1938

George Peabody was born in Columbus, Georgia. After their general store business was ruined in the Civil War, his family moved to Brooklyn, New York, in 1865. Peabody attended Deer Hill Institute for a few months, but he credits the Brooklyn YMCA for his education. He would go there at night to read in their library. He befriended Spencer Trask and became a partner in Trask and Stone. He worked there for twenty-five years and amassed a sizeable fortune because of his skill at railroad, mining, and utilities management during the "Gilded Age." He helped develop Edison Electric Illuminating Company, which later became General Electric. He retired in 1906 at age fifty-four and devoted the rest of his life to philanthropy.

Peabody had extensive forest land holdings. While he never attended the University of Georgia, he felt it represented the best of his native state and showered it with gifts. He gave $50,000 for the Peabody Library (now Hunter-Holmes Administration Building) and

$60,000 for a University World War I memorial, which became Memorial Hall. He endowed the internationally renowned George Foster Peabody Awards for recognition of excellence in electronic media journalism. These highly coveted awards are now administered by the UGA Henry W. Grady College of Journalism and Mass Communication and are awarded each year at a ceremony at the Waldorf-Astoria Hotel in New York.

Peabody was an early and strong advocate for minority education. He was treasurer of the national Democratic Party, and he served on the Board of Directors of the Federal Reserve Bank of New York for eight years. Peabody was a close friend of President Franklin D. Roosevelt and worked with him to make Warm Springs, Georgia, a health center. He founded Yaddo, an artists' retreat near Saratoga Springs, New York. He received honorary degrees from UGA, Harvard, and Washington and Lee, and he was a life trustee of the University of Georgia.

Peabody had a close attachment to the University and was a great friend of University Chancellor Walter B. Hill. It was through that friendship that Peabody gave the gift that established the George Foster Peabody School of Forestry. It retained that name until 1968. George Foster Peabody was a man of humble beginnings who proved himself in a crucible. Most importantly for Georgia forestry, he never forgot his roots, and we are all better off because of his vision.

Charles Holmes Herty
1867–1938

Charlie Herty was born in Milledgeville. He graduated from the University of Georgia in 1886 with a Ph.B. degree. He took his Ph.D. in chemistry from Johns Hopkins in 1890. That same year, he became an assistant in UGA's Chemistry Department. As an early indication of his well-rounded life, Herty introduced football to the University of Georgia campus and became its first football coach.

Herty got his earliest ideas about the cup-and-gutter system while studying in Zurich, Switzerland. He spent some time in Germany and had seen the French cup-and-gutter system. Herty's cup-and-gutter method of tapping trees was based on that methodology.

In 1902 Gifford Pinchot, legendary chief of the U.S. Forest Service, hired Herty away from the University of Georgia as an "expert." In early autumn of that same year, Herty presented a paper, "Apparatus for Collecting Crude Turpentine," at a Turpentine Operator's Association meeting in Jacksonville, Florida, and the turpentine industry was turned on its head. He had based his paper on experiments he conducted in Ocilla. The new method saved southern forestry, replacing the inefficient, destructive "box" system for gathering gum. Landowners who switched to his method began to get higher gum lease rates, trees reached maturity in a sounder condition, and natural reproduction rebounded. Thus, the seeds of the pulp and paper industry's wood basket were sown. "Revolution" is a modest word to describe what this meant to Georgia forestry, but another bigger revolution was in the wings, standing on the shoulders of this one.

In 1927 Herty visited the extensive pinelands of Alex Sessoms near Cogdell. He saw the reproducing forest of young trees and decided a market must be developed for them. Based on preliminary research, the Georgia General Assembly funded a laboratory in Savannah for Herty to develop a pulp and paper market for southern yellow pine. His subsequent research and production using the sulfate process demonstrated that newsprint and kraft paper could be made from Georgia pines. The first run in 1933 was used to print an edition of the *Soperton News* from trees grown by Jim Fowler in Treutlen County. This discovery turned the pulp and paper establishment on its head, and the face of southern forestry was changed forever.

For his numerous achievements, Herty was widely honored by his profession, the University of Georgia, and the state of Georgia. Herty Drive and Herty Field are named in his honor, the latter being the site of Georgia's first gridiron. He was elected to membership in the Sphinx

Club. The Savannah Pulp and Paper Laboratory was renamed for him, and a street on the Georgia Southern University campus bears his name. In the Georgia Capitol, there is a bronze tablet citing his significant role in starting the pulp and paper industry in Georgia. Charles Holmes Herty was a savior and champion of Georgia forestry in particular but southern forestry in general.

Alfred A. Akerman
1876–1962

Dean Akerman was born in Cartersville. His father was attorney general in the Grant administration. He graduated from the University of Georgia's Franklin College in 1898 and received his M.F. from Yale University in 1902. He briefly studied forestry at the University of Tuebingen in Germany. His work experience before coming to Georgia included what was then the USDA Bureau of Forestry and teaching assignments at Yale and Syracuse. He was state forester of Connecticut for only one month before becoming state forester of Massachusetts until 1906.

After Peabody gave money to found a school to specifically benefit rural Georgians, Akerman threw himself into forming the new school and extending knowledge to private

landowners—all while he was the only staff member. His students affectionately referred to him as "Daddy" Akerman, possibly because of his paternal interest in them. He helped found the Forest Club, and when he resigned, he was presented with one of its newly minted green and gold membership pins.

In addition to fulfilling his numerous duties as professor and Extension agent, Akerman quickly acted to found the Georgia Forestry Association a few months after the Forestry School was dedicated. He very wisely saw the need for an effective, statewide organization that could be an advocate for the School as well as forestry in Georgia. Peabody, Hill and Barrow had the vision; Akerman followed through on it.

After he left Georgia in 1914, he joined the faculty at the University of Virginia and became director of its Seward Forest. He retired as professor emeritus of forestry in 1950. His papers were donated to the University of Virginia library upon his death.

Jim L. Gillis, Sr.
1892–1975

Jim L. Gillis, Sr., was born in Emmanuel County. "Mr. Jim," as he was affectionately known, was born into a forestry family. His father, Neil Lee Gillis, was a pioneer in forestry. Neil, with his brother, Murdoch Gillis, co-founded Soperton Naval Stores Company in 1890. Jim graduated from the University of Georgia in 1916. He immediately started farming and began working for Soperton Naval Stores in 1927.

"Mr. Jim" was an early member of the Georgia Forestry Association, and he served on its executive committee in 1931. He continued to expand his prosperous naval stores business and became the largest landowner in Treutlen County. Later, with his timber background and political influence, he was in an ideal position to continue promoting the interests of Georgia's burgeoning forest industry.

Gillis was elected to the Georgia General Assembly House of Representatives right out of college, in 1916. He was the youngest person ever to serve in the General Assembly at that time. Later, he served in the State Senate and was elected president pro tempore. "Mr. Jim" served as Treutlen County ordinary from 1934 to 1936.

He is best known for his longtime, legendary leadership of the State Highway Department. He was first appointed to the then three-person State Highway Board by Governor E. D. Rivers in 1937. He continued his service under four more governors. In his position as state highway director, he oversaw the paving of many rural "farm to market" roads, which helped promote agriculture, forestry and economic development. He is the man who got Georgia "out of the mud" and into a system of modern

highways and bridges. He served as state highway director longer than anyone and became a major political force during his long public service. He served as chairman of the Georgia Democratic Party in the 1930s and was responsible for all presidential patronage in the state. He and U.S. Senator Herman Talmadge were close friends, and that further helped promote forestry, which both men admired. Interstate Highway 16 is named in Gillis' honor.

Bishop F. Grant
1897–1970

Professor Grant, affectionately known by the students as "The Bull of the Woods," was born in Wallhalla, South Carolina. Grant served in the U.S. Army's 30th Division in France during World War I. He received his B.S.F. and M.S.F. degrees from Georgia in 1925 and 1933, the second master's awarded. He was a member of Alpha Zeta and Phi Kappa Phi national scholastic honorary fraternities. After working for a lumber company in Georgia, Florida, and South Carolina for two years and in nursery work for two years, he was appointed adjunct professor of forestry in 1929 and became a permanent faculty member in 1933. He served two different terms as interim dean.

For thirty years, he was director of the Sophomore Summer Camp, mostly held at Hard Labor Creek State Park. The "hard labor" was not a misnomer, as he broke in the new class of would-be foresters each summer. He was noted for being a hard taskmaster and for wearing his honor society keys on a watch chain in his vest even in summer.

Following Dean Weddell's death in May 1956, he very ably served as interim dean until the selection of Dr. Al Herrick as permanent dean in 1957. He was revered by generations of students, alumni and colleagues as an outstanding teacher and humanist. He was elected to the inaugural class of the Georgia Foresters Hall of Fame in 1969. In 1976, the School named its largest experimental forest in his honor.

"Bish's" influence extended well beyond the School. His service was sought after on many University committees, and he was a staunch defender of the University. A favorite quote of his regarding detractors of the University was, "Don't worry about those folks. The University was here a long time before they came and will be here a long time after they leave."

William M. Oettmeier, Sr.
1898–1975

Bill Oettmeier, Sr., was born in Pittsburgh, Pennsylvania. After serving in the Marine Corps during World War I, he graduated from Penn State University with an honors forestry degree in 1926. His experience with the Marine Corps exposed him to the use of field radios under combat conditions. He used that experience to pioneer the use of radios as a forestry communication device especially for firefighting. Superior Pine Products Company was the first forestry concern to get an FCC radio license for radio use in firefighting. This one advancement alone was literally a life saver for many future forest fire-fighters nationwide.

Superior Pine Products Company was incorporated in 1925 as a subsidiary of Paper Makers Chemical Corporation. SPP hired Oettmeier, Sr., in 1926. After "Cap" Eldridge left Superior Pine to head up the USFS southern forest inventory program, Oettmeier was promoted to Suwannee Forest manager in 1932 and later president in 1946. He went back into the service as an officer in the Army Air Corps in the

Pacific Theater of Operations during WWII. He was on the fifth plane that landed in Japan right after the surrender.

In these early years in the flatwoods he began to see the need for forest owners to become better informed and organized. Oettmeier became the driving force behind the establishment of the Forest Farmers Association in 1941. Bill Sr. met Judge Langdale on a train to Washington, D.C. The judge was going to a meeting called by the Forest Service to discuss the future of private forestry. The judge asked Bill to go along, and at the meeting about private landowners Oettmeier saw there were none to be found. He resolved to remedy the situation so private forest owners would have someone to speak for them. Oettmeier founded the Forest Farmers Association and served as its president and as president of GFA. He was elected to the Georgia Foresters Hall of Fame.

While SPP had about twenty-five crops of turpentine boxes and a sawmill, Bill Sr. saw the end of the turpentine business and the rise of the pulp and paper business. He negotiated a long-term lease with Rayonier, but that fell through. He eventually negotiated a highly favorable sixty-year cutting lease with St. Regis Paper Company in 1947. That served as the model for all other landowner-friendly long-term leases.

His hard work, dedication, and vision are still paying dividends for private forest owners.

Harley Langdale, Jr.
1914–

Harley Langdale is a living legend. He comes from a forestry family, which has seen seven generations care for the forests of South Georgia. As chairman of the board of the Langdale Company, he built up a small turpentine business so that he now oversees the operations of twenty separate companies with well over a half billion dollars in gross income. The influence he has had in the positive evolution of forestry in the nation is amazing. Forest owners throughout the nation can thank him for his pivotal role in securing capital gains tax treatment of timber, expanded markets for pulpwood, and financial backing for investment in reforestation and purchasing cut over timberland, to name a few. One of his favorite quotes is, "Our success is people."

Harley graduated from the George Foster Peabody School of Forestry in 1937. As a student, he led the now famous "student revolt," which resulted in the School getting a new building, modern textbooks and raises for faculty. Harley and nine other students went directly to Governor E. D. Rivers and pled their case for increased funding for the School. After the visit, the Board of Regents caved in, and the

School was set on its current path to national excellence. He recounts that the "revolt" was not without its testy moments with the chairman of the Regents and the president of the University, but he says it was worth it. That was just a taste of what his leadership would do.

Through the years, Harley has expanded the company founded by his grandfather, and in so doing he has rendered a great service to forestry. He holds Georgia Registered Forester License Number 3, and he has been an active leader in every facet of the state, regional and national forestry community. He has served as president of the Georgia Forestry Association and Forest Landowners Association. He has been honored as Man of the Year by the National Forest Products Association, Georgia Foresters Hall of Fame, GFA Wise Owl Award, Warnell School of Forestry and Natural Resources Distinguished Alumnus Award and is an honorary member of AGHON.

Harley Langdale, Jr., is the definition of a forester.

Archie Edgar Patterson
1915–2004

Professor Patterson was born in Boone, Iowa. He obtained his B.S. and M.S. degrees in forestry from Iowa State University in 1937 and 1938. He joined the faculty of the George Foster Peabody School of Forestry in 1940. He resigned to serve in the U.S. Army as a staff sergeant in the European Theater of Operations in World War II.

For forty-one years, he taught hundreds of undergraduate and graduate forestry students forest management, forest management planning, forest policy, forest law, ethics and leadership. He was affectionately known as "Prof" by all who knew him. That was short, of course, for professor, but it also was for "professional." "Prof" was the ultimate professional. He always wore a coat, tie and hat and preached that your knowledge alone would not make you a professional—you had to look and behave professionally, too. He was an untiring supporter of forestry professionalism and professional societies. He was vice president of the Society of American Foresters, SAF Council member, Southeastern Section chairman, Georgia Division chairman, and a fellow of SAF. He served on the University of Georgia Executive Committee for a number of years and through several crises.

He pushed for the licensing of foresters for many years. Finally in 1951, a bill he wrote passed virtually unchanged in the Georgia General Assembly. With its passage, Georgia became the first state to have a forestry registration law. He served for ten years on the Georgia State Board of Registration for Foresters and was its chairman. He was elected to Gridiron, AGHON and the Georgia Foresters Hall of Fame.

Patterson was also renowned for his insistence on ethical practices. He taught and practiced them well. His "Four Ethical Tests" are still the simplest distillation of what ethical practice in any profession ought to be. He lectured on professionalism and ethics at gatherings throughout the nation even after retirement. Archie Patterson was the "conscience of the forestry profession."

James L. Gillis, Jr.
1916–

"Jim L." is a forester, business executive, public servant, banker, timberman, cattleman, and farmer. He has been very active in conservation work as long as he can remember. A native of Soperton, Jim L. graduated from the University of Georgia with a B.S. degree in forestry in 1937.

His family has long been in the timber business. He worked briefly for the Georgia Forestry Commission in Baxley before joining his family's Soperton Naval Stores, Inc., in 1938. Through the years, Gillis has gained the respect and admiration of all those who have done business with him in the management of his 12,000 acres of timberland and his community service.

It is his service to his profession and state that truly distinguishes him as a complete professional and gentleman. He serves on the boards of the Georgia Forestry Association, Georgia Forestry Commission, and Bank of Soperton. He was the longtime president of the American Turpentine Farmers Association and past president of GFA, the Georgia Bankers Association, and Association of County Commissioners of Georgia. Jim L. has received numerous awards for his contributions and service to these diverse groups.

While he claims no interest or inclination in politics, Jim L. served one term as a Georgia state senator, was a Treutlen County commissioner for forty years (chairman 1973–2001), was on the Soperton City Council, was Soperton mayor for five years, and served several Georgia governors in varying capacities.

His lifelong love has been forestry and its role in the state. He is the longest-serving GFC commissioner in history, having been appointed in 1977. He has been reappointed by every governor since then. His devotion to the Commission is evident by his tireless work as its chairman since 1981. He was elected to the Georgia Foresters Hall of Fame in 2002.

Hugh M. Gillis, Sr.
1918–

Hugh Gillis is a wonder. No person in United States history has served as

a state legislator longer than Senator Gillis. He was first elected to the Georgia House in 1940 at age twenty-two. He served that body for twelve years until he was elected to the State Senate in 1956. He retired as a senator in 2004 after more than fifty-five years'* service to Georgia.

Hugh was born in Soperton into a farming and forestry family. He graduated from the University of Georgia with a B.S. degree in agriculture in 1940. He got into the family farming, turpentine, and timber business at the same time. During all his years in public office, he never forgot about forestry and agriculture or rural Georgia. Those were the things that renewed and inspired him. For those who witnessed him in legislative action, it was easy to see he never wavered in his support of forestry. He was especially instrumental in the passage of House Resolution 836, which placed Amendment Number Three on the ballot in 1990, amending the Georgia Constitution to give family farms and forests long-sought relief from crippling property taxes.

Hugh was one highly respected lawmaker and great supporter of health and education issues. He was Senate president pro tempore for six years and served as chairman of the Senate Corrections, Appropriations, and Natural Resources and Environment Committees during his long tenure. His last service was as the longtime chairman of the Natural Resources and Environment Committee, where he helped oversee the passage of numerous bills supporting forestry and environmental quality. He was a man you could trust at his word and who could exercise tremendous power for the greater good of Georgia.

He still serves as president of Gillis Ag and Timber, vice president of Soperton Naval Stores, Inc., and is a member of the Georgia Ports Authority. He received GFA's Wise Owl Award and is an honorary member of AGHON.

Hugh's service does not add up to sixty-four years because the County Unit System of elections before 1962 rotated State Senate seats among the various counties in a Senate district.

Leon Abraham "Buddy" Hargreaves, Jr.
1921–1997

Buddy Hargreaves was born in Pearson, a suburb of Waycross. He played basketball for two years at South Georgia College. His education was interrupted in March 1943 by WWII after a short term in the Forestry School. Hargreaves served as a sergeant in the U.S. Army Infantry and saw action in Italy, where he developed his management credo: "Never be the first one out of the foxhole." He was and got blown back in! Many years later, Buddy received the Bronze Star Medal for heroism under fire and the Purple Heart. He spent several months convalescing in England. He returned to the University in January 1945 and completed his stellar student undergraduate career. He was campus leader, president of the student body and a member of Gridiron, Blue Key, ODK, Alpha Zeta, Xi Sigma Pi, and

AGHON. He earned his B.S.F. and M.S.F. degrees in 1946 and 1947. Later, he obtained his M.P.A. and Ph.D. degrees from the University of Michigan in 1953.

Hargreaves worked for UGA as instructor from 1949 to 1954. Then, he became assistant director of GFC from 1954 to 1960. He was assistant woodlands vice president for St. Regis in Jacksonville, Florida, from 1960 to 1966. He returned to his alma mater in 1966 as a full professor and associate to the dean. Buddy became dean in 1980 and was elected fellow of the Society of American Foresters in 1981. He helped write legislation creating the Georgia Forest Research Council, and he was its director for a brief period. He used his influence to establish a research funding mechanism for the School through GFRC. He was a noted expert on taxation of timber land and arbitration. Hargreaves was instrumental in bringing the U.S. Forest Service Forest Science Laboratory to campus. It was the first time a Forest Service lab was located on a state university campus. He received GFA's Distinguished Service Award in 1970, the Order of the Golden Pine Cone. AGHON presented him the AGHON Award in 1971 and 1977, and he served as AGHON's ritual master from 1966 until his death. He was SESAF chairman and chairman of the Clarke County Board of Tax Assessors. As research coordinator for the School, he was able to significantly increase its federal funding base.

Hargreaves was renowned as a hard-nosed administrator, and more than one University president was scared of him. He set down his management philosophy in his amusing *Red Eye Rules of Administration*. There was reason to fear him if you were a bumbling, intractable "North Campus bureaucrat," but if you got on his good side through brilliance and/or hard work, he was a complete pushover.

As dean, Hargreaves led the highly successful 1985 Bicentennial capital campaign, which significantly increased the School's endowment in land, cash and buildings. The campaign was so successful that the University borrowed $1 million dollars from the School at a Hargreaves-negotiated high interest rate. He labored for seventeen years to secure state appropriations for Forest Resources Building Four. He finally achieved this goal in 1989 and retired two years later not guilty of "statutory senility."

Charlie Bonner Jones
1924–

Charlie Bonner Jones, one of forestry's most colorful leaders, was born in Milledgeville, Georgia. He began his college career at Georgia Military College, but that program was interrupted —as it was for so many—by World War II. He served his country as a staff sergeant in an infantry machine gun company in the European Theater of Operations. He was wounded in action in France and was decorated with the Purple Heart.

After the war, Bonner came to Athens to begin his degree work. It was during this time that he formed a lifelong deep friendship with fellow wounded veteran and forestry classmate, Buddy Hargreaves. Bonner says he was Hargreaves' "nursemaid." He graduated with a B.S.F. degree in 1948 and began his civilian career as assistant district forester for the Georgia Forestry Commission in Macon. After two years there, he worked for McElrath Lumber Company when it had more than 80,000 acres of forestland. He then worked twelve years for Dixie Wood before starting his own business, Oconee Wood, in 1963. In 1970, he formed J & H Timber Company in Milledgeville, and was a loyal Union Camp wood dealer for more than twenty-five years. He is still in the consulting business for major Georgia piedmont landowners.

"Bad Bonner" developed that moniker for his determined work to enhance the profession of forestry. He was often ribbed about his dogged determination, but that was always with the deepest respect for his efforts. He was elected to the Georgia Foresters Hall of Fame, named a fellow of the Society of American Foresters, and presented with GFA's highest award, the Wise Owl. Jones served his profession as chairman of the Ocmulgee Chapter, Georgia Division and Southeastern Section of the Society of American Foresters; and he received the SESAF Excellence in the Practice of Forestry Award. He is past president of GFA, past president of the Warnell School of Forestry and Natural Resources Alumni Society, and the second Big Jayhook of the Jayhole Club. The School of Forestry and Natural Resources presented him with the Distinguished Alumnus Award in

2005. Jones served on the University of Georgia Alumni Society Board of Governors, the Georgia Military College Board of Directors, and GMC Foundation Executive Committee.

Two things stand out in Bonner's distinguished career. The first is his hard and often underappreciated work in 1983–84 to change truck weight laws in Georgia. He remembers being in the Speaker of the House's conference room in the state capitol with a DOT negotiator. Speaker Murphy locked them in and told them they could come out when they reached an agreement. They did, and log truckers are much better off because of Bonner's hard-nosed bargaining.

His second labor of love for forestry has been his long service on the Georgia State Board of Registration for Foresters. He was first appointed in 1979 and is still serving. He became the institutional memory of the Board and served for many years without compensation as Board enforcement officer. "Old Bonner" is a true champion of forestry.

L. N. "Tommy" Thompson, Jr.
1925–1999

Lawrence "Tommy" Thompson was born in Mount Vernon, Georgia. He enlisted in the U.S. Navy in 1943 and served two years on active duty

during WWII. Following service, he completed his degree in forestry from the University of Georgia and received a master of forestry from Duke University in 1950. As a classmate of Bonner Jones and Buddy Hargreaves, he developed a lifelong commitment to the School of Forestry and Natural Resources.

Tommy's early work experience was with Tidewater Plywood, W. B. Byrd Lumber, Gilman Paper Company, and Georgia-Pacific. He worked for G-P for twenty-one years in positions of increasing trust and responsibility in forest management, logging and lumber manufacturing until he became its general manager of the Southern Division. He helped increase G-P's land holdings significantly and was an early leader in the development of the southern plywood industry. He left G-P as its head of Florida operations.

He soon founded T & S Hardwoods in Milledgeville in September 1973. He patiently built that business from a small capitalization to a $20 million operation with several hardwood sawmills. He was also involved with international forestry projects in Chile and Brazil. Tommy was known as an innovator, a shrewd businessman and strong supporter of forestry. When Windsor Castle Great Hall burned in 1993, it was T & S Hardwoods that supplied the Georgia oak beams for reconstruction. Tommy was a master at hardwood silviculture and a tireless proponent of scientific forest management and responsible stewardship. He was a member of the Board of Visitors of the Duke School of Forestry and Environmental Studies, a University of Georgia Foundation trustee, a charter member of the Center for

Forest Business Advisory Committee, a director of the Hardwood Manufacturers Association, GFA, and the Century Trust Bank.

Thompson was honored for his distinguished service to forestry by being elected to the Georgia Foresters Hall of Fame and was named Warnell School of Forestry and Natural Resources Distinguished Alumnus in 1994. Tommy took great pleasure in a special service he rendered to the state and international community in 1996. He was mostly responsible for the rough production of 10,000 Georgia pecan handles for the 1996 Olympic torches. Tommy was a Georgia forest treasure.

Eley C. Frazer III
1926–

Eley Frazer was born in Lafayette, Alabama. He attended Auburn from 1946 to 1948 and graduated from the University of Florida with a B.S.F. degree in 1950. Frazer co-founded F&W Forestry Services in 1962 and has been instrumental in its growth and development into a highly respected leader in forest resource management in the South. Prior to co-founding F&W, Frazer served as an area forester for the Florida Forest Service and in the woodlands operations of St. Joe Paper

Company. While in school he operated a logging business.

He served as operating partner of F&W until 1967 when he was named president, remaining in that position until 1988 when he became chairman. As chairman, Frazer maintains an active role in the management of F&W and serves as the company's chief real estate appraiser. He is a recognized authority on forest policy and tax issues and has testified numerous times before committees of the U.S. Congress. He has held top leadership positions in state, regional, and national forestry professional and industry groups.

A Fellow in the Society of American Foresters, Frazer has held leadership positions in the Forest Landowners Association, Association of Consulting Foresters, Georgia Forestry Association, Florida Forestry Association, and Georgia Board of Registration for Foresters. He served a fourteen-year term as a member of the Georgia Forestry Commission, and chaired the Forest Industries Committee on Timber Valuation and Taxation. Eley received GFA's Wise Owl Award in 1985. He was inducted into the Georgia Foresters Hall of Fame in 1994, and was named Distinguished Forester by the Association of Consulting Foresters that same year. In 1995, he received the Forest Farmer of the Year Award.

Eley Frazer has never been one to back down from an argument, and forestry is better off because of that "bulldog" trait. He is known as an energetic, involved and outspoken forestry advocate for the private landowner. Frazer has been tireless in his landowner advocacy, community efforts and business endeavors. Jack

Warren, former FLA executive vice president and fierce Georgia Bulldog, used to fondly introduce Eley as "an Auburn dropout and Florida graduate." Eley Frazer may not be a Bulldog, but he has firmly established himself as a preeminent forester of national renown and a great Georgian.

Jerome L. Clutter
1934–1983

Born in Washington, Pennsylvania, and raised in Pittsburgh, Professor Clutter received a B.S. in forest resources from Michigan State University in 1956 and a master of science and doctor of forestry from Duke University in 1957 and 1961, respectively. While his early years were spent with the USFS as the Southern Experiment Station statistician, Jerry spent over twenty years on the faculty at the University of Georgia in a teaching and research role where he was Union Camp professor of forest management. He taught a generation of foresters about basic mensuration, growth and yield, and the importance of rational forest planning techniques. Recognized on many occasions by students and the University as an outstanding teacher and mentor, Jerry loved the art and science of forestry and teaching it to students.

A pioneer in the field of biometrics and quantitative timber manage-

ment planning, Jerry founded the Biometrics and Operations Research Unit of the University of Georgia. This group continued to grow and became an important component of the University's School of Forestry and Natural Resources. Dr. Clutter taught classes and mentored graduate students in the School of Forestry and Natural Resources and in the Franklin College's Statistics Department.

His contributions to the biometrics and growth and yield literature are many, including the development of compatible whole stand growth and yield models, the derivation and use of diameter distribution based growth and yield models, and the use of linear programming in forest management planning. For these research activities Jerry was widely recognized as a contributing researcher in the fields of growth and yield and forest planning. Dr. Clutter was named a National Science Foundation Fellow and received the U.S. Department of Agriculture Certificate of Merit for his research activities.

Through his work with the Society of American Foresters, Dr. Clutter was heavily involved in SAF science policy development during a time of increasing awareness of forest resources management. He served as the chair of the SAF Forest Sciences Board along with several appointments to the Forest Science Editorial Board. He was elected to the Georgia Foresters Hall of Fame and Gridiron Club.

Working with others at the School of Forestry and Natural Resources and the forest products industry in the South, Jerry guided the creation and development of the Plantation

Management Research Cooperative—an organization that investigated the impacts of forest management activities on the growth, yield, and stand structure of pine plantations. This cooperative is still in existence and provides data and information on the pine plantation resource in the South.

Those who knew Jerry appreciated his engaging wit and straightforward approach to both research and teaching. For many students he took a challenging and at times, intractable, subject and was able to present it in novel and understandable ways. He enjoyed being a teacher.—*By Dr. Mike Clutter, UGA Center for Forest Business*

Williamson S. "Bill" Stuckey
1935–

Bill Stuckey is a native of Eastman, Georgia. He graduated from the University of Georgia with a B.B.A. in 1956 and L.L.B. in 1959.

In 1966, he was elected to represent Georgia's 8th Congressional District in the United States Congress. At the time, the 8th District was the most heavily forested Congressional District in the U.S. He served five

terms and retired from public life in 1976. While in Congress, he was instrumental in the passage of two major environmental bills affecting Georgia's natural resources. The first of these laws was a law placing the Okefenokee Swamp into the National Wildlife Refuge and Wilderness Act. This gave additional protection to one of the nation's largest wetland ecosystems. The second law was the naming of Cumberland Island as a National Seashore.

As a congressman, his love of the land, kindled by his father, was firmly rooted. After his legislative tenure, Bill devoted himself to several family business interests including the management of Stuckey Timberland, Inc. He became involved in GFA and the Forest Landowners Association. He served as president of FLA and was named its Forest Landowner of the Year in 1999. His service to FLA was marked by his special interest and influence in the legislative arena. He helped organize an effective grassroots effort to help push passage of several bills of service to small forest owners.

Bill has also been recognized for his service to the University of Georgia and his community with the Blue Key Service Award. In working for forest landowners, Bill has always determined to bring wisdom, moderation and stability to the debate. His strategy has proven to be a winner, as he is.

William M. Oettmeier, Jr.
1938–

Bill Oettmeier, Jr., was born in Valdosta. He grew up in the company forestry town of Fargo and graduated in 1960 with a B.S.F. degree in forestry from the University of Georgia. He started his remarkable forestry career in LaGrange with St. Regis Paper Company in 1960. He was assistant regional manager and helped set up St. Regis' Monticello, Mississippi, pulpmill operations in 1965. While in Monticello, he was elected to the City Council. He served six years in the Georgia Air National Guard as an airman second class.

Oettmeier has the very unusual distinction of being the only person to serve as president of the Forest Landowners Association twice and as president of GFA twice. After his initial term as GFA president, where he had to break in a new executive director from Ware County, he was called again to serve. During the severe illness and incapacitation of the current president, Leon Hargreaves, and with GFA having lost its sitting vice president to a company transfer, Oettmeier was easily talked into becoming GFA acting president because he consented while partially sedated in the hospital himself.

Bill's service to forestry, his state, and community are unparalleled. He has been president of the Georgia Division of SAF, helped found the Flatwoods SAF chapter, serves on the Board of the Georgia Sheriff's Boys Ranch, served on the Georgia Forestry Commission Board, served as the forestry representative on the Advisory Board of the Federal Reserve Bank of Atlanta for three years, and served on the Governor's Education Reform Task Force. He is a SAF fellow, member of the Georgia Foresters Hall of Fame, Warnell School of Forestry and Natural Resources Distinguished Alumnus, Past Big Jayhook, AGHON member, and Wise Owl recipient.

Bill Oettmeier is a humble man and works in quiet ways. Most people would never know that, at his own expense, he hosts an annual Georgia Sheriff's Boys Ranch "Boys Hunt" for severely abused boys. This is more than just a couple of hours on a deer stand. It is a once-in-a-lifetime opportunity for these boys to be guided one-on-one by stars from sports, television, and rock 'n' roll. They could be hunting with an Olympic gold medalist, All-Pro NFL lineman, *Dukes of Hazzard* regular, Hall of Fame baseball great, or Rolling Stones keyboardist. These men all say that it is the "once in a lifetime" experience for them to be asked to participate. Bill does it all and has been quietly but duly honored for his humanitarian efforts.

An Oettmeier has been working for Superior Pine Products Company for more than eighty-one years. Bill Oettmeier is one of those foresters who come along once in several generations. He has made an indelible, bright mark on forestry. Bill is a modern renaissance man: he is a first-rate forester; an excellent hunter, fisherman and golfer; a painter; ardent supporter of public education; a steady leader; and a master politician. His is a trail marked with glory that few will be able to follow.

Charles M. Tarver
1945–

Charley was born in Mobile, Alabama. He is a 1968 graduate of the School of Forestry and Wildlife Sciences at Auburn University, where he has served on the Advisory Council and Development Committee. The University named him Outstanding Alumnus in 1992.

Tarver is a decorated Vietnam veteran and served as a pilot in the U.S. Air Force.

Charley has been in the timberland investment business since 1979 and pioneered that business for tax-exempt institutions, beginning with the development of the country's first pooled timberland investment fund while employed at the First National Bank of Atlanta. This concept changed the face of forestland investing nationwide. Charley is the founder, president and CEO of Forest Investment Associates, a registered investment advisor, headquartered in Atlanta. The firm specializes in timberland investment management for large institutional investors, and it manages more than 1.5 million acres with a market value in excess of $2 billion.

He is a registered forester with experience in banking and finance. He serves on the board of directors of the Longleaf Alliance, is a member of the Society of American Foresters and serves on its Investment Committee. Tarver is also a member of the Association of Consulting Foresters and is past president of the American Forestry Association, the nation's oldest citizen conservation organization. He helped form and is past chairman of the Forest Landowners Tax Council. Charley has served on the boards and executive committees of the Georgia Forestry Association and the Forest Landowners Association. Charley Tarver is a man of vision and principle.

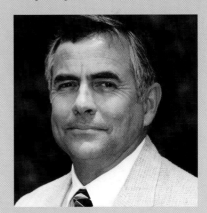

William Eugene Lancaster
1949–2003

Billy Lancaster was born in Forsyth, Georgia. He graduated with a B.S.F.R. from the University of Georgia in 1971—in the class the stars fell on. He was a solid student and forged lifelong friendships while at Georgia. Early in his career, he worked for Kendrick and Associates and Georgia Kraft. He then moved to the equipment sales side of forestry where he truly excelled as a forester and manager. He was METRAC's Forestry Equipment Division manager at his death.

Billy was a true servant leader. He always unselfishly gave of his time and resources to better his profession, community and state. He served as president of the Warnell School of Forestry and Natural Resources Alumni Association and the Forsyth Lions Club. He was a member of the GFA Board, and he chaired the Georgia Division, Society of American Foresters. He was widely recognized for his contributions by being named Warnell School of Forestry and Natural Resources Distinguished Alumnus in 2002 and by being elected to the Georgia Foresters Hall of Fame in 2003. He received the Soil and Water Conservation Merit Award and Coalition for a Green Georgia Outstanding Achievement Award.

In the application of knowledge and service to forestry, he was recognized as a leader in the development and implementation of outstanding forestry safety and equipment programs. His expertise was highly respected and valued.

However, his outstanding dedication to promoting forestry was best demonstrated through his leadership in founding the Georgia Division SAF Youth Camp. By recognizing the need for youth to understand the importance of forest resources in their daily lives, Billy convinced his fellow foresters a Youth Camp was the right idea. He served as chair

and treasurer of the Forestry Youth Camp Fundraising Committee from 1988 to 2003. He made the time commitment it took to attend every single Youth Camp.

Through his sustained leadership, hundreds of Georgia teens gained awareness and knowledge of the value of forest resources to the economy and their lives, as well as a keen appreciation of the forestry profession.

Billy Lancaster was a true friend, dedicated spokesman for forestry, and professional role model.

Charles A. "Chuck" Leavell
1952–

For those who don't know his forestry roots, Chuck Leavell would seem a highly unlikely champion of forestry. But he is that and more. Chuck was born in Tuscaloosa, Alabama, and began his music career right after high school. He is most famous for his continuing role as keyboardist and music director for the Rolling Stones, with whom he has been affiliated since 1982. Chuck is a well respected and highly sought-after artist, and he has performed with Eric Clapton on his multi-Grammy award winning *Unplugged* album, B. B. King, Aretha Franklin, George Harrison, Sea Level, the Allman Brothers Band, the Indigo

Girls, the Black Crowes, the Fabulous Thunderbirds and a host of others. He has released his own works on the *Forever Blue: A Piano Solo* and *Southscape* titles. Chuck has been inducted into the Georgia Music Hall of Fame as well as the Alabama Music Hall of Fame. After thirty years in the music business, he has established himself as a proven star.

His wife Rose Lane's father and grandfather were farmers and also tended their family forests. When she inherited the family farm near Bullard, Georgia, that responsibility fell on their hands, and they moved to what was called "The Home Place." They have never left. It was here that Chuck began his love affair with the land. It got into his soul as much as music had. He knew he had to learn more. So while touring with the Fabulous Thunderbirds, he completed a Forest Landowners Association forestry correspondence course. He was hooked, and he enrolled in the American Tree Farm program. From there, he became a GFA member and was involved in the successful 1990 Amendment Three campaign. He is GFA and American Tree Farm spokesman and serves on their committees. Chuck and Rose Lane were selected as Georgia Tree Farmers of the Year in 1990 and 1998 and became National Tree Farmers of the Year in 1999. Leavell received the National Arbor Day Foundation Good Steward Award for his dedicated public service, and he has been honored by the Georgia Conservancy, AGHON, American Forest Foundation, U.S. Department of the Interior, FFA and many others. He is an honorary alumnus of the Warnell School of Forestry and Natural Resources where he and his wife have endowed the Chuck and Rose Lane Leavell Scholarship.

He felt so deeply about forestry that he wrote the beautiful *Forever Green: The History and Hope of the American Forest,* which speaks so eloquently about the need for balance in conservation and is now in its second edition and has been translated into German. Chuck always seems to have time to host Project Learning Tree groups, Landowner Field Days and other similar events or speak about his passion for forestry. When he does, he is usually enticed to render his stunning versions of *Georgia on My Mind* and *Georgia Pines.* His life's credo has been, "My family, my trees and my music."

Alva Joe Hopkins, III
1952–

Joe Hopkins was born in Folkston and grew up in the family timber business. He developed a love of the land and respect for landowner rights as he rode with his father and Uncle Harold Gowen along the sandy roads in and near the Okefenokee Swamp. This understanding of sweat equity helped Joe formulate his desire to maintain the family holdings and make them better. He saw it took a lifelong commitment to truly practice forest conservation and that at many times the rewards were long in coming.

His formal education was not exactly the preparation one would expect of someone who might one day try to look after the family forest and fight ticks and mosquitoes. Joe received his A.A. degree from Oxford College and his B.A. from Emory University. As he left Emory, he was told that maybe he was best suited for a career as a football coach. Nevertheless, he got his J.D. from Walter F. George School of Law at Mercer University, and actually passed the bar examination the first time. From 1977 to 1988, Joe was in the private practice of law in Charlton County. During this time, he began to ease into management responsibilities with one of the family businesses, Toledo Manufacturing Company, Inc. Finally, he made the switch to full time management of the family forestry business. He is president of Toledo and serves on the boards of Hopkins-Gowen Oil Company, Inc., Southeastern Bank and Gowen Timber, Inc. Hopkins was a founding member of the internationally recognized federal, state, and private firefighting partnership—the Greater Okefenokee Landowners Association (GOAL).

As he became more involved in forestry matters and less in trials, Hopkins immersed himself in various forestry groups including the Georgia Forestry Association and Forest Landowners Association. He quickly got on the GFA Board then executive committee and served as president in 1997. Joe is now on the Forest Landowners Board and is a Georgia Forestry Foundation trustee.

Hopkins became very active in forestry issues with the Amendment Three ad valorem tax campaign of 1990 and the years beyond when enabling legislation was passed and refined. He attended hearings, gave testimony, made speeches and stumped like a true politician. During this time, Joe developed and nurtured his deep feelings on balancing government needs with private property rights. He became an ardent, fervent proponent of not sacrificing landowners' private property rights to bureaucrats. With a skillful style and a message from the heart, he started to get attention and respect for his "out-of-the-mainstream" ideas. Even a secretary of the interior listened. The result is a wider acceptance of balance for private landowners and a radically changed federal endangered species policy. He saw a problem, and with his typical bulldog style he latched on to it until he got a response. Very few others had the courage to buck the tide and make something positive happen.

Warnell School of Forestry and Natural Resources

Warnell School of Forestry and Natural Resources Deans

Alfred A. Akerman
1906–1914

James B. Berry
1914–1920

Thomas D. Burleigh
1920–1930

Gordon D. Marckworth
1931–1939

Donald J. Weddell
1939–1956

Allyn M. Herrick
1957–1980

Leon A. Hargreaves, Jr.
1980–1991

Arnett C. Mace, Jr.
1991–2002

Richard L. Porterfield
2004–

Jayhole Club lapel pin.
Courtesy WSFNR

Jayhole Club

The University of Georgia Chapter of the Jayhole Club was founded October 15, 1976, on Whitehall Forest. National headquarters was specified to be the "Dog House Room" of Whitehall Forest in possible reference to the infamous "dog house" the School of Forestry and Natural Resources was in 1937. The stated objective of the Jayhole Club is "to promote the well-being of the University of Georgia and its School of Forest Resources."[1]

The Jayhole Club was founded in 1976 to provide a resource base of well connected alumni and friends who could be called upon from time to time to help the school. When the normal system of pushing the school's goals breaks down or is otherwise frustrated, the Jayhole Club is called upon to provide relief and problem resolution.

In the early days of logging in the mountains, loggers came up with a unique method of snaking logs downhill. A team of mules or horses would be hitched up to a log or turn of logs. The animals would then snake the load straight down the hill. The laws of nature being constant, if the slope of the mountain and weight of the logs combined to create a speed greater than the speed at which the animals were toiling, a vexing problem occurred.

Now, loggers, being as resourceful as they are, figured out that something extra was needed above and beyond normal logging techniques. Their solution was simple, elegant, and very workable. First, they dug a turn-out every so often down the slope. This turn-out was dug in the shape of a "J." If the load got going too fast, the team master simply turned the team into the J-shaped hole in the ground. Problem one was solved. Next, the logger had to keep the load from following into the Jayhole or snatching the team out. Again, a simple device known as a "Jayhook" was attached to the harness. A simple flick of the wrist would release the Jayhook and separate animal from load.

When the dean, faculty, and administration are taking their "logs" downhill on gentle slopes, the Jayhole Club is not needed. However, when the slopes get rough and the problems outrun the problem solvers, the Club gets the nod to act as a Jayhole for the School. The formal name is Concilium Pro Excellentia Scholae Silvarum, which means "Council for Excellence in the Forestry School."[2]

Student Organizations

AGHON Society

Founded in 1920, AGHON is the highest honor a student in the College of Agricultural and Environmental Sciences, Warnell School of Forestry and Natural Resources, or College of Veterinary Medicine may attain while at the University of Georgia. Its purpose is "to honor leadership, character and extracurricular activities."[3]

Ag Hill Council

The Ag Hill Council was founded in 1941 to support funding for a South Campus student center. The idea died, but the group lives on and now serves as the coordinating body for all Ag Hill student clubs including those of the Warnell School of Forestry and Natural Resources, the College of Veterinary Medicine, the College of Agricultural and Environmental Sciences, and the College of Family and Consumer Sciences.

Forestry Club

The Forest Club was founded February 4, 1914. Burley Lufburrow, Class of 1915, was elected as the first president. Courtland Winn, Jr., Class of 1915, was elected secretary.[4]

Forestry Club members, 1997. *Courtesy WSFNR*

At the club's second meeting on February 11, 1914, a committee was formed to design a suitable pin.[5] The official name of "The Forest Club of the University of Georgia" was adopted on April 1, 1914.[6] The Honorable Henry Solon Graves, chief of the U.S. Forest Service, was guest speaker on April 14, 1914, and he was elected as the first honorary member.[7]

The minutes of an autumn 1914 meeting contain a rough drawing of the club pin, and mention was made in the minutes about writing people about the pin.[8] The March 16, 1915, minutes reference a motion passing to buy a pin for Professor Akerman. So, the pin must have been made between October 1914 and this meeting, although no official reference is made about it being made

Top right: Founding minutes of the Forestry Club, 1914. *Courtesy WSFNR*

Right: The first Forestry Club membership pin from 1914. *Donated by Courtland Winn, Jr., of Atlanta (2005). Courtesy Steven A. Brown, citation: Forestry Resources Estrays, UGA 85-033:1, folder 11*

and available. Secretary Courtland Simmons Winn, Jr.'s, hand-written note in the University of Georgia Hargrett Rare Book Room Forest Resources Estrays collection with the original pin must be in error because he dates the pin to 1913, which was at least a year before the Forest Club was founded.[9]

GEORGIA WINS FIRST ANNUAL CONCLAVE OF SOUTHERN FORESTRY SCHOOLS

by David Brantley

Three top photos are *courtesy of WSFNR*

School of Forest Resources student patch designed by Mitch Flinchum, 1969. *Courtesy Bob Izlar*

Forestry Club patch from 1990s. *Courtesy Bob Izlar*

The Club must have been in decline in 1917–18, possibly due to World War I, because the only reference in the Forest Club minute book is a simple listing of the officers for that academic year.[10] The next minutes are from November 10, 1920, and they mention the purpose of the meeting was to reorganize the club.[11] They again appointed a committee to design a club pin.[12] The committee offered a pin in the shape of a red gum leaf with "F.C." and "U.G." being borne on the leaf lobes. The club finally approved this design at its October 12, 1921, meeting, but no further reference is made to the pin, nor are there any known copies or pictures.[13]

The first student publications at the School were by the Forestry Club members, but in later years the School annual was jointly published by the Forestry Club, Wildlife Society, and Xi Sigma Pi. These

UGA Conclave participants with Peavy Hook, ca. 1950s. *Courtesy WSFNR*

publications are a great resource of pictures and articles about student life, the status of the School and forestry in general. They cover most of the School's history from 1916 to 1972 when the burden of another extracurricular activity became too much for the faculty advisor and publication was shut down after the 1972 edition. The general format of the editions from the 1920s through the mid-1950s had student and faculty pictures; campus scenes; poems about trees, faculty, students, and various dreaded courses; stories about summer camp or internship experiences; as well as interesting articles by alumni or potential employers on employment and pressing forestry issues of the day. After the middle fifties, the *Cypress Knee* became more of a small version of the University annual, the *Pandora*.

The first of these was *Forest Club Annual*, released in 1916. Its theme was "Conservation of Natural Resources in Georgia," and the entire issue was devoted to it. The

students told nothing of their motivation for publishing an annual, although later years' clubs noted the yearly volume was meant to be a memorial to that year's senior class. This "Conservation" issue provided an excellent review of world and local forest conditions with numerous high-quality pictures and testimonials from three former U.S. presidents, university presidents, practicing professionals, and the like.

The 1917 edition's theme was "Georgia Forest Trees" and was sold for 25 cents. This issue was dedicated to Georgia's school children and is essentially a dendrology text of important trees. The students still made no mention of their activities or interests other than thanking advertisers and faculty members.

There is no record of a publication after 1917 until the 1923 *Cypress Knee* appeared. No mention was made of the reason for the hiatus, but perhaps it was World War I or some other reason. There is mention in the 1928 volume that the forestry club was

reorganized in 1920 after a "period of inactivity."[14] Perhaps this time of inactivity by the club contributed to the cessation in publication.

While there is no allusion to how the *Forest Club Annual* became the *Cypress Knee* in the inaugural edition, the 1929 volume has this to say:

This little book, the 'Cypress Knee,' may be compared to those out in the swamp, it has all their beautiful ideals, ambition, and purposes. Its life also is one of service, lifting itself above all difficulties and opposition so it may help the strong trunk of the forest school raise its many branches of work above the cold, murky waters which retain its growth out into the sunlight, so many students may enjoy happiness and success.[15]

In the 1928 yearbook, the Forestry Club's purpose was explained: "The Forestry Club is an organization fostered to promote good feeling and fellowship among the students of the Forestry School to furnish relaxation, well spiced with instructive talks on subjects of interest either directly or indirectly connected to Forestry."[16]

The club was reorganized in 1920 after several years of dormancy. This may account for the lack of an annual from 1919 to 1923. No doubt the Great War [1917–18] had some effect. The Forestry Club may have been "unofficially" involved in publication of Summer Camp news logs. The mimeographed 1939 Summer Camp Log of the camp held in Olustee, Florida, gives a day-by-day [nights, too!] description of typical summer camp curricular and extracurricular activities.[17] Tommy Blalock did a "cleaner" summary of the 1959 Sophomore Summer Camp at Hard Labor Creek State Park.[18]

Alpha Xi Sigma

The University of Georgia Gamma Chapter of the national forestry honorary fraternity Alpha Xi Sigma was founded at the School on February 16, 1926, after students repeatedly petitioned the mother chapter at the Syracuse School of Forestry. Apparently, the Syracuse members had felt Georgia had too few students to sustain a chapter.

Charter members were John B. Gaskins, Lewis E. Fitch, Charles P. Doherty, E. Bauer, and Charles W. Nuite. Gaskins was elected the first chief forester. The Georgia chapter was first mentioned in the 1928 *Cypress Knee*. It was last mentioned in the 1941 edition, and the 1942 volume mentions that Xi Chapter of Xi Sigma Pi national honorary forestry fraternity was chartered at Georgia May 23, 1941.

Alpha Xi Sigma's purpose and ideals were stated thus in the 1928 yearbook:

The aim and purpose of this fraternity is to promote a higher standard of scholarship among forestry students, and it is hoped that a greater number of those who are enrolled as students in the profession of forestry will strive hard to gain this honor. We hope that the objective will not be for the honor alone, but through greater effort during their years in college, they will be better fitted for practical service.[19]

Xi Sigma Pi

A brief mention was made by student Bishop F. Grant in 1925 about the possibility of chartering a chapter at Georgia of the national forestry honorary, Xi Sigma Chi. Could he have meant Xi Sigma Pi, which, having been founded at the University of Washington in 1908, was active at the time?[20] Xi Chapter was chartered at Georgia in 1941 with the able assistance of "Prof" Archie Patterson. It is still on campus. Xi Sigma Pi seeks to honor academic achievement and high character of students in all majors of the School. Georgia's Xi Chapter had the 1956–58 National Officer slate consisting of Dr. Lyle Wendell Redford Jackson, forester; Professor Bishop F. Grant, associate forester; and Professor J. Reid Parker, secretary-fiscal agent.[21]

The Wildlife Society[22]

The University of Georgia Student Chapter of the Wildlife Society was formed in 1967. Dr. Fred Evenden, then executive secretary of the Wildlife Society, presented the charter to Bob Bridges, student chapter president, on May 9, 1968. There were forty-seven charter members.

Historically, the Chapter has averaged around thirty members, but in recent years membership has climbed to well over fifty members.

Top left: Xi Chapter, Xi Sigma Pi logo, 1999. *Courtesy Deek Cox*

Left: Georgia Gamma Chapter charter for Alpha Xi Sigma, national honorary forestry society fraternity, 1926. *Courtesy WSFNR*

Top: Graduate student Clay George with American Oyster Catcher, 2001. *Courtesy WSFNR*

Bottom: Wooden phoenix carved by Mitch Flinchum, 2005. *Courtesy WSFNR*

The dues-paying membership for the 2004–05 academic year was eighty-four. Meetings are held twice per month during the school year and consist of a business meeting and a presentation by a guest speaker.

Annual events of the chapter include a fall venison burger picnic to welcome new members, participation in the wildlife competition at the annual Association of Southern Forestry Clubs' [ADFC] Conclave, and participation in the Southeastern

Wildlife Students' Conclave. The biggest event of the year is the annual Wildlife Supper. The first Wildlife Supper [then called the "Buzzard Banquet"] was held in January 1968. Attendance at the supper has grown steadily, and approximately 200 to 300 people now attend. The supper, which is now held in late April or early May, is the major fundraising event for the chapter.

The first Southeastern Wildlife Students' Conclave was held in 1972 in Tennessee. Initially, the Conclave was held in conjunction with the Annual Conference of the Southeastern Association of Game and Fish Commissioners.

The 1974 and 1975 conclaves were cancelled when the Association selected meeting places at expensive resort hotels in states outside the boundaries of the Southern Section of the Wildlife Society and without a suitable and willing host school. The conclave was then reorganized to meet independently of the Southeastern Association beginning in 1977 at Auburn University, and the date was changed from fall to early spring. The UGA Chapter has attended every conclave.

The UGA chapter won the first Quiz Bowl competition held in conjunction with the 1972 Wildlife Students' Conclave and has done very well in wildlife competitions since that time. In 1973, UGA finished third in the Quiz Bowl, being narrowly beaten in the semifinals by Mississippi State University. Confusion over rules and an unexpected preponderance of fisheries questions were factors in the loss. In 1978, graduate students were not allowed to participate, and the UGA team [with only three members] failed to place in the top three. [Current rules allow two graduate students on the four-student team.] UGA hosted the Conclave in 1980 and 1990 and was ineligible to compete in the Quiz

Bowl. Of the thirty Quiz Bowls UGA has participated in, they have won thirteen times, placed second three times, and placed third three times.

Student Chapter, Society of American Foresters

The students organized themselves as an affiliate of the Georgia Division of the Society of American Foresters in the 1940s but did not receive an official charter until 1984. The Student SAF Chapter has been very active through the years. The students often meet with the Oconee Chapter, and each year student representatives have attended Division, Southeastern Section and national SAF meetings. The Georgia Division and Southeastern Section each sponsor scholarships for student SAF members. Every winter, the Chapter hosts the "SAF Roundtable" for employers and perspective employees. The Chapter has a long history of supporting the Forestry Club and Forestry Conclave.

American Fisheries Society, Georgia Student Chapter

The mission of the American Fisheries Society is to improve

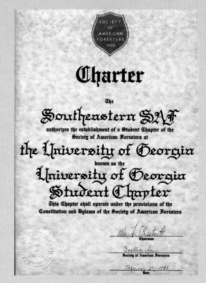

Left: Student Chapter, SAF, on wetlands tree planting project, 2000. *Courtesy Brian Stone*

Fisheries student, 2000. *Courtesy WSFNR*

the conservation and sustainability of fishery resources and aquatic ecosystems by advancing fisheries and aquatic science and promoting the development of fisheries professionals.

Student Chapter, Soil and Water Conservation Society

The student chapter was founded in 2004. The national organization serves as an advocate for conservation professionals, science-based conservation practice, programs and policy. The Georgia student chapter is focusing on wetlands restoration projects and elementary school outreach.

American Water Resources Association, Georgia Section, UGA Student Chapter [23]

Originally started in the early 1990s, the chapter has hosted a number of meetings and events over the years. Chapter membership is predominantly from Forestry and Natural Resources, with additional members from Engineering, Ecology, Crop and Soil Sciences, Geology, Geography, Environmental Design, and a wide range of other programs. The club participates in annual community outreach events designed to involve citizens in monitoring and improving local rivers and streams. They host monthly meetings, open to members and other interested students, which familiarize students with current water resource issues and careers. They assist with

functions related to the Georgia Water Resources Conference, and they also raise funds to assist with travel and other experiences that benefit the professional development of members in the field of water resources.

Graduate Student Association

The Graduate Student Association represents graduate students and works with the faculty and Graduate School to address any issues the students may have. GSA hosts the very popular "Graduate Research Symposium" each spring.

Warnell School of Forestry and Natural Resources Student Clubs and Advisors 2005–2006

American Fisheries Society

President: Jeff Ziegeweid
Vice President: Pete Hazelton
Secretary/Treasurer: Jessica Skyfield
Advisor: Aaron Fisk

Soil and Water Conservation Society

President: Adam Speir
Vice President/Treasurer: Matt Miller
Officer at Large: Scott Stanfill
Advisor: Larry Morris

Graduate Student Association

President: Jason Nedlo
Vice President: Scott Rush
Secretary: Audrey Owens
Treasurer: Libby Mojica
Advisor: Ron Hendrick

UGA Forestry Club

President: Coby Smith
Vice President: Jason Carey
Firewood Vice President: Max Lang
Secretary: Adam Speir
Treasurer: Sara Johnson
Conclave VP: James Kent
Advisor: Pete Bettinger

The Wildlife Society

President: Lindsey Kirkman
Vice President: Jason Norman
Secretary: Daniel Van Dijk
Treasurer: Emily Brown
Advisors: Steven Castleberry/Mike Mengak

Xi Sigma Pi

Forester: Jay Chupp
Vice President: Andrew Saunders
Ranger: Emily Brown
Treasurer: Josh Agee
Advisor: Bob Izlar

Student Chapter SAF

Chairman: Jason Carey
Co-Chairman: Jerry Mahon

Fall 1988 class. *Courtesy WSFNR*

Fall 1996 class. *Courtesy WSFNR*

Secretary: James Kent
Treasurer: Adam Speir
Advisors: Dick Daniels/Bob Izlar

American Water Resources Association

President: Josh Romeis
Vice President: Justin Welch
Secretary: James Grecco
Treasurer: Noah Fraser
Advisors: Rhett Jackson/Todd Rassmussen

WSFNR Student Ambassadors 2005–2006

Graduate Students

Tyler Clemons
Jan Forrest
Jason Nedlo
Scott Stanfill
Christie Stegall
Justin Tyson
Sharon Valitzski
Ryan Whitelaw

Undergraduate Students

Justin Brooks
Emily Brown
Jason Carey
Bob Carlson
Jay Chupp

Modern-day student practicing prescribed burning, ca. early 2000s. *Courtesy WSFNR*

Sara Johnson
James Kent
Daniel Meyran
Andrew Saunders
Adam Speir
Evan Sussenbach
Daniel Van Dijk
Michael Westbrook
Alan Zeigler

Faculty

Dr. Bruce Beck
Dr. Pete Bettinger
Mr. Larry Biles
Dr. Bruce Borders
Dr. John Carroll
Dr. Steven Castleberry
Dr. Chris Cieszewski
Dr. Michael Clutter
Dr. Kim Coder
Dr. Michael Conroy
Dr. Robert Cooper
Dr. Sarah Covert
Dr. Coleman Dangerfield
Dr. Richard Daniels
Dr. Jeffrey Dean
Dr. David Dickens
Dr. Aaron Fisk
Dr. Mary Freeman
Dr. Dale Greene
Dr. Gary Green
Dr. Gary Grossman
Mr. Tom Harris
Dr. Ronald Hendrick
Mr. William Hubbard
Mr. Kris Irwin
Mr. Bob Izlar
Dr. Ben Jackson
Dr. Rhett Jackson
Dr. Cecil Jennings

Georgia lumber ready for the market. *Courtesy TLC*

Transgenic eastern cottonwood plantlets growing in tissue culture, ca. 2005. *Courtesy WSFNR*

Dr. Peter Lasier
Dr. John Maerz
Dr. Daniel Markewitz
Dr. Brooks Mendell
Dr. Michael Mengak
Dr. Scott Merkle
Dr. J. Michael Meyers
Dr. Karl Miller
Dr. Clint Moore
Dr. Dave Moorhead
Dr. Larry Morris
Dr. Joseph Nairn
Dr. David Newman
Dr. Nate Nibbelink
Dr. Douglas Peterson
Dr. James Peterson
Dr. Richard Porterfield,
   Dean
Dr. Todd Rasmussen
Dr. Laurie Schimleck
Dr. Sara Schweitzer
Dr. James Shelton
Dr. Jacek Siry
Dr. James Sweeney
Mr. Paul Sykes
Dr. Michael Tarrant
Dr. Robert Teskey
Dr. Bob Warren
Dr. Parley Winger
Dr. Richard Winn

Staff

Henry Ayers
Douglas Bagby
John Bagby
Sara Baldwin

Forests provide clean water.
Courtesy GFA

Forestry Complex courtyard, ca.
2000s. *Courtesy WSFNR*

Kara Baker
Angela Barber
John Bates
James Baxter
Joyce Black
Kurt Bogenrieder
John P. Bond
Jay Brown
Molly Brown
Patrick Bussell
Goulet Carruth
Eileen Carroll
Daniel Cassidy
Sandra Cederbaum
Mark Cherry
Eugene Crouch
Rebecca Cull
David Clayton
Eva Dalton
Gisele (Andrade) Dean
Jason Derifaj
Michelle Dillard
Peter Dimmick

WARNELL SCHOOL OF FORESTRY
AND NATURAL RESOURCES
100 Year
CENTENNIAL

Ingvar Elle
Todd Elsbernd
Chris Fonnesbeck
Brian Fosgate
David Gaines
Donna Gallaher
Glynis Habeck
Doug Hall
Bridget Harden
Mike Harrison

*"Georgia Pines, Georgia Pines. How
I miss that home of mine."* Lyrics by
the Candymen, 1967. *Photo courtesy
Plum Creek*

Matthew Head
David Higginbotham
Angela Holliday
Chris Holliday
Fred Holman
Brenda Howard
Jay Howell
Matthew Howell
Michael Hunter
Johnny Hutchens

Top: White Hall, 2005. *Courtesy WSFNR*

Inset: White Hall staircase, 2005.
Courtesy WSFNR

Kwang-Seuk Jeong
Jesse Johnson
Tina Jones
J. B. Jordin
Bonnie (Fancher) Kepler
Shane Kornberg
Allyson Lawrence
Gail Lebengood
Jimmy Lee
Walt Lorenz
William Lott
Eric Lowe
Tripp Lowe
Gail Lutowski
Eugene MacIntyre
John Mackert
Doug Marshall
Michael Marsh
Sarah Martin
Salina McAllister
Mary McCormack
Bryan McElvany
Mary Anne McGuire
Tavis McLean
Krista Merry
Christie Miller

Mary Mitchell
Frank Mohone
Paul Montello
Kevin Murdock
Michael Murphy
Anthony Myrick
Amanda Newman
Morgan Nolan
Michelle Norris
Lee Ogden
David Osborn
Suzanne Paschal
Jimmy Dale Porterfield
Diane Pritchett
Rosetta Raburn
Bob Ratajczak
John Rheney
John Ruiz
Malissa Russell
Holly Rutledge
Joe Sanders
Jennifer Schleis
Michael Segars
John Seginak
Dean Shirley

Kathy Simmons
Anuj Sinha
Allen Smith
Rick Smith
Dustin Thompson
Sunnie Toole
Barbara Trotter
Jeffery Turner
Lisa Vaughan
Chieh-Ting Wang
Mingling Wang
Byron Whitener
Daniel Williams
Randall Williams
Rosemary Wood
Alicia Wood-Jones
Elaine Wright
Jenny Yearwood
Jianping Zhu
Steven Zimpfer

Warnell School of Forestry and Natural Resources Distinguished Alumnus Award Recipients

1993	W. N. "Hank" Haynes
1994	L. N. "Tommy" Thompson
	Harley Langdale, Jr.
1995	Dr. Forest E. Kellogg III
1996	John W. Mixon
1997	Robert L. Izlar
1998	James Gowen Fendig
1999	Frederick W. Haeussler
2000	Frederick W. Kinard, Jr.
2001	J. Reid Parker
2002	William E. "Billy" Lancaster
2003	Frank Montfort Riley, Jr.
2004	Frederick C. Gragg
2005	Charlie Bonner Jones

Warnell School of Forestry and Natural Resources Distinguished Young Alumnus Award Recipients

1999	George Michael Zupko IV
2000	William Mark Ford
2001	Todd H. Mullis
2002	Scott P. Jones

Effie's brick placed in Flinchum's Phoenix fireplace chimney, 2005. *Courtesy WSFNR*

2003   Dr. Michael Alexander Menzel
2004   None
2005   Wendi Weber

Warnell School of Forestry and Natural Resources Board of Advisors

Capital Campaign & Development Committee

Jim Alfriend
Dennis Carey
Sam Dollivar
Kenneth Gibson
Jim Hickman
Forest Kellogg
Fred Kinard
Syd Kinne
Bill Miller III
Tom Norris
Jane Rodrigue

Flinchum's Folly with "totem pole" name post in Whitehall Forest, Homecoming 1976. *Courtesy WSFNR*

Earl Smith
Don Taylor
Burke Walters
E. J. Williams
Len Woodward
Faculty & Staff
David Newman
Mike Clutter

Mike Hunter
Bob Izlar
Mary McCormack
Jim Sweeney

Forest Lands Committee

Wayne Barfield
Dan Forster
Bill Guthrie

Flinchum's Phoenix, 2005. *Courtesy WSFNR*

Billy Humphries
Chuck Leavell
Ken Stewart
Andy Stone
Faculty & Staff
Mike Hunter
Dan Markewitz
Sara Schweitzer

Legislative Committee

Earl Barrs
Forest Kellogg
Scott Jones
Wesley Langdale
Steve McWilliams
Tom Norris
Colin Myerson
Faculty & Staff
Bob Izlar
Todd Rasmussen

Investments

Tommy Fulghum
Forest Kellogg

Bob Leynes
Kate Robie
Blake Sullivan
Tom Trembath
Faculty & Staff
Mike Clutter
Dick Porterfield
Anuj Sinha

Center for Forest Business

John Anderson
Jon Caulfield
Jim Fendig
Kenneth Gay
Bruce Hansen
Bill Miller III
Tom Reed
Earl Smith
Jody Strickland
Don Taylor
Marshall Thomas
Jim Webb
Faculty & Staff
Bob Izlar
CFB Faculty

Alumni Steering Committee (elected)

Fred Allen
Earl Barrs
Mike Harris
Rob Olszewski
Robert Pollard
Mike Smith

Georgia white-tailed deer. *Courtesy GFA*

ESTABLISHMENT
CEREMONIES

G. NORMAN BISHOP
ARBORETUM

JAN. 1966

WHITEHALL FOREST
JANUARY 29, 1966
11:00 A.M.

Top: Dedication announce-
ment for the G. Norman
Bishop Arboretum, 1966.
Courtesy WSFNR

Left: Mary Kahrs Warnell Forest
Education Center. Dedicated
November 7, 2001, Guyton,
Georgia. *Courtesy WSFNR*

Andy Stone
E. J. Williams
Brian Wommack
Len Woodward
Stephen Worthington
Mike Zupko

Faculty & Staff

Bridget Harden
Mary McCormack
Dick Porterfield

Instruction & Outreach Committee

Jim Alfriend
Lindsay Boring
Steve Chapman
Mark Ford
Tim Lowrimore
Jim Rundorff
Peter Stangel

Faculty & Staff

Dick Daniels
Ben Jackson
Bob Warren
Susan King

Ex-Officio

David Newman
Jim Sweeney

Young Alumni

Nolan Banish

Andy Barrs
Mary Gresham
Greshelda Hazelton
Alex Menzel
Liberty Moore
Tom Reinert
Carol Guy Stapleton
Brian Stone
Rans Thomas
Sharon Valitski
Heather Venter

Faculty & Staff

Mary McCormack
Amanda Newman
Dustin Thompson

Warnell School of Forestry and Natural Resources Alumni Association Steering Committee 2005

Earl Barrs	*President*
Mike Zupko	*President Elect*
Andy Stone	*Past President*
Bridget Harden	*Secretary*
Fred Allen	
Mike Harris	
Rob Olszewski	
Robert Pollard	
Mike H. Smith	
E. J. Williams	

Brian Wommack
Len Woodward
Stephen Worthington

Flinchum's Folly and Flinchum's Phoenix[24]

David Mitchell Flinchum's M.S.
thesis in 1971 used several site
plans incorporating water resources,
vegetation, soils, wildlife, and
viewsheds. As a case study in his
work, he used a model to be built on
the North Oconee River. The area
selected was near an old mill site
that had ceased operations in the
1940s. There was a rock wall raceway
and old mill foundation that was
proposed as the foundation of the
recreational building. His site plan
included the building, bridges to a
river island, hiking trails, parking,
and playing fields. The work also
included floor plans and elevations
that were mostly faithfully followed
in the actual construction.

Mitchell selected a twelve-acre site
located on the west bank of the
North Oconee River. Flinchum's
design of a pavilion, meeting
rooms, kitchen, and restrooms was

Daniel Brooks Warnell
1881-1945

Daniel Brooks Warnell was a native Georgian who was involved in the management of banking, farming, and timber enterprises. He served in the Georgia House of Representatives from 1931 to 1937 and in the Georgia Senate from 1937 to 1939. As a state legislator, Mr. Warnell made significant contributions in rural development, public education, public transportation, and management of forest resources.

Mr. Warnell made a significant contribution to the forest industry, when in 1938, he supplied some pine for the work of chemist Charles H. Herty. This led to the discovery that southern pine could be used for the manufacture of paper pulp, thus making possible one of the South's most important industries.

The School of Forest Resources was dedicated in honor of the late Daniel B. Warnell in 1991.

Daniel Brooks Warnell, 2005. *Courtesy WSFNR*

constructed in 1972 with funding from alumni and friends of the School. Flinchum's Folly was built on the rock foundation of the old mill. It became *the* meeting place for student clubs and alumni. Unfortunately, it burned November 13, 1977, after a student club had met there. They had a fire in the fireplace, but it was put out before they left. The chimney was completely inside the building, and there is speculation that a spark got through a chink in the mortar and started a smoldering fire inside. When the students came back the next morning to clean up, the place was gone. Support from students and alumni poured in, and Flinchum's Phoenix was built on a high bluff overlooking the confluence

of the North and Middle Oconee Rivers. The site is on land donated to the School by the grandchildren of Nat D. Arnold. The gift consisted of seventeen acres and included an abandoned electric power plant and dam. The Phoenix was dedicated April 20, 1979.

History of the Georgia Cooperative Fishery Research Unit[25]

The Georgia Cooperative Fishery Research Unit was established on October 11, 1962, under joint sponsorship of the Bureau of Sport Fisheries and Wildlife (now Fish and Wildlife Service), the Georgia Game and Fish Commission (now Georgia Department of Natural Resources, Wildlife Resources Division), and the University of Georgia. Since its beginning forty years ago, the Unit has been instrumental in performing research for its cooperators and other resource agencies, providing for the education and training of students, and publication of research results in professional outlets.

The Unit has always been housed within the School of Forest Resources, University of Georgia, which provides office, laboratory, storage, and other research space. Since 1964, the Unit has utilized ponds and research space at the 750-acre Whitehall Forest, which is located about five miles from campus. A new laboratory/office facility at Whitehall Forest was occupied by the Unit in 1967, the same year in which new Unit main offices were completed in the Forestry School's six-story research addition on campus. In the past,

Unit staff and students have frequently utilized other space and facilities both on and off-campus during the course of cooperative research with University faculty and other agencies. Off-campus facilities have included Sapelo Island Marine Institute, Fort Gordon Military Reservation, Savannah River Plant, and a variety of labs, refuges, and hatcheries operated by state and federal cooperators.

History of the Wildlife Cooperative Research Unit[26]

The Cooperative Research Unit System started in Iowa. The thrust for the start of this program was the work of one individual, Jay Norwood "Ding" Darling. Ding Darling was a nationally famous editorial cartoonist and an ardent, well-informed natural resources conservationist.

Ding Darling became the chairman of the Iowa Fish and Game Commission in the early 1930s. He quickly began working with a few other conservationists of the time to relieve what he saw as utter devastation to fish and wildlife resources. The Depression had hit hard, and the lack of concern or regulations for the use of fish and wildlife resources since the great westward movement in the United States had resulted in the wholesale destruction of habitats and fish and game populations directly. Market hunting was going full tilt, and the extinction of the once numerous passenger pigeon had already occurred because of it. Darling recognized what was happening to the fish and wildlife resources, being used to benefit a few greedy citizens when, in fact, our constitution guarantees public ownership of these resources for the benefit and enjoyment of all citizens. When Darling sought to find ways to better manage these resources and to have the public laws enforced, he quickly found that there was an acute shortage of information of the kind needed to manage fish and wildlife resources, and that there were no biologists trained to perform the necessary research to develop the needed information.

In 1934 Darling was appointed by the secretary of agriculture (Henry Wallace, another Iowan) to serve as the chief of the Bureau of Biological Survey. By the 1935–36 school year, Darling had secured federal funding to place a biologist at each of eight additional state Land Grant colleges and thus established the first wave of cooperative wildlife research units, cooperatively funded by state, university and federal funds.

Several minor changes have occurred in the supportive arrangements, but the basics have withstood the test of time. (1) Fishery units were added in the early 1960s to specifically address fishery problems (prior to this, the wildlife units did some fishery research). (2) In the mid-sixties, assistant leaders were authorized for research units. (3) In the early 1980s, the FWS agreed to work toward combining the separate fishery and wildlife units into three-person combined fish and wildlife units to meet the Reagan Federal Austerity Program guidelines. All new units are being formed as three-person combined units. (4) The program has proved to be highly effective and popular.

Warnell School of Forestry and Natural Resources Milestones

BSF 1912—Josiah Tattnall Kollock
BSF 1916—Burley Mathew Lufburrow (fourth graduate)
MSF 1932—George Norman Bishop
MF 1950—Robert Walter Cannon
PhD 1964—William Roy Sizemore
1951—Dick Mordecai, University valedictorian
B. M. Lufburrow and B. B. Lufburrow, WSFNR's first father/son graduates[27]

Dedications[28]

School of Forestry Facilities Golden Anniversary Celebration, October 6, 1956

School of Forest Resources and Forest Sciences Laboratory Dedication, September 28, 1968

G. Norman Bishop Arboretum, January 29, 1966

Bishop F. Grant Memorial Forest, April 23, 1976

Mary Kahrs Warnell Memory Garden, April 12, 1991

L. L. "Pete" Phillips Wood Utilization and Plant Sciences Building, April 25, 1991

Eva Thompson Thornton Memory Garden, May 28, 1991

Forest Resources Building Four, October 9, 1993

Mary Kahrs Warnell Forest Education Center, November 7, 2001

CENTER FOR FOREST BUSINESS
Warnell School of Forest Resources
UNIVERSITY OF GEORGIA

Top: UGA Bicentennial Quilt, 2005.
Courtesy WSFNR

Bottom: WSFNR Lobby, 2005.
Courtesy WSFNR

Georgia Forestry Association, Inc.

appendix three

Georgia Forestry Association, Inc., Board of Directors 2005

Jeff Alexander	Georgia Forest Products, Inc.
James I. Alfriend	J. I. Alfriend Consulting Foresters
Joe Allen	Southeastern Wood Producers Association
Kathleen Atkinson	USDA Forest Service
Deborah Baker	Georgia-Pacific Corporation
Charles Balfour	Balfour Pulpwood Company, Inc.
Earl Barrs	Knapp-Barrs and Associates, Inc.
Barry Bedingfield	Quality Forest Products, Inc.
Lawrence Bennett	Alma Exchange Bank & Trust
Nipper Bunn	Bunn Logging
Chris Cannon	Flint Holdings
Dennis L. Carey	Pine Timber Company
Steve Carter	Tolleson Lumber Company, Inc.
Linda Casey	International Paper Company
Dave Christopher	Trus Joist
Steve W. Crawford, Jr.	Steve Crawford Forest Products
Charles D. Daniel	Wachovia Timberland Investment
Walt Dasher	Dasher Industries
Laura Devendorf	Melon Bluff Plantation
Dave Dodge	New South Companies, Inc.
Steve Duda	Bowater, Inc.
Johnny Floyd	Floyd Timber Company, Inc.
David Foil	Forest Resource Consultants, Inc.
David A. Francis III	Francis Forestry Services
Eley C. Frazer III	Eley C. Frazer Consulting Forester
Larry Fudge	Langdale Industries, Inc.
Cheryl George	Packaging Corporation of America
Kenneth Gibson	Temple-Inland Land & Timber, Inc.

GFA headquarters conference room, 2005. *Courtesy GFA*

Hugh Gillis, Jr.	Gillis Ag & Timber
Jim L. Gillis, Jr.	Soperton Naval Stores, Inc.
John Godbee	F & W Forestry Services
W. Dale Greene	Warnell School of Forestry and Natural Resources
Bill Guthrie	Weyerhaeuser Company
Robbie Haranda	AgSouth Farm Credit, ACA
Rullie Harris	Weyerhaeuser Company
Allen Hodges	Hodges Land & Timber, Inc.
Alva Joseph Hopkins III	Toledo Manufacturing Company
H. Ed Hutcheson	Georgia Timberlands, Inc.
Bob Izlar	Warnell School of Forestry and Natural Resources
Steve Johnson	Thompson Hardwoods
C. Bonner Jones	J & H Timber, Inc.
Sam P. Killian III	Past President
J. Wesley Langdale III	The Langdale Company
Harley Langdale, Jr.	The Langdale Company
Bob Leynes	Canal Wood, LLC
Robert Luk	Temple-Inland
Gene Martin	Georgia-Pacific Corporation
Al Massey	International Paper Company
Gary McMahan	Canal Wood, LLC
William F. Miller III	Past President
David K. Mitchell	Past Tree Farm Chairman
John W. Mixon	John W. Mixon & Associates, Inc.
Paul Mott	Past President
John Mullis	J. M. Huber Corporation
Colin Myerson	Superior Pine Products Company
Tom Norris	Interstate Paper/Newport Timber
Jim O'Connor	Gum Swamp Woods, LLP
William M. Oettmeier, Jr.	Superior Pine Products Company

Jekyll Island, Georgia, has been the site of many GFA annual meetings. *Courtesy Plum Creek*

Joe Parrott	Rayonier
Joe Parsons	Smurfit-Stone Container Corporation
David Pattison	Graphic Packaging
L. O. "Pete" Peebles, Jr.	Peebles Timber, Inc.
Robert W. Pollard, Jr.	Pollard Lumber Company, Inc.
Donald E. Pope	Packaging Corporation of America
Richard "Dick" Porterfield	Warnell School of Forestry and Natural Resources
H. Wayne Ragland	Gainer & Ragland, Inc.
Pat Reddish	Interstate Paper/Newport Timber
Lee Rhodes	Rhodes Timber Company
Frank Riley	Scofield Timber Company
Tom Ritch	Southern Heritage Land Company
Harold Rozier	International Paper Company
James Rundorff	Plum Creek Timber Company
Richard V. Saunders, Sr.	Alexander Brothers Lumber Company
Michael T. Shearer	Global Forest Partners, LP
Monte Simpson	MeadWestvaco
John H. Sisson	Sisson Realty & Timber Services, Inc.
Ben Smith	MeadWestvaco

GFA headquarters, Forsyth, Georgia, 2004. *Courtesy GFA*

W. Earl Smith	Gilman Building Products Company
Jerry Spillers	Smurfit-Stone Container Corporation
Ken Stewart	Georgia Forestry Commission
Andy Stone	Stuckey Timberland
Blake Sullivan	Sullivan Forestry Consultants, Inc.
Bobby Taylor	Past President
Robert Terrell, Jr.	T & T Timber Company
Marshall D. Thomas	F & W Forestry Services, Inc.
Tom Trembath	Forest Investment Associates
Skipper Van Cleave	Valley Wood, Inc.
Andrew J. Vann	Plantation Forestry, Inc.
William F. Varn	Varn, Inc.
Larry Walker	Past President
Glen Warnock	Gay Wood Company, Inc.
Carlton L. Windsor	Rayonier
Stephen F. Worthington	Rayonier
Claude Yearwood	The Price Company
H. G. Yeomans	Yeomans Wood & Timber
Kurt Zweizig	T & S Hardwoods

GFA Past Presidents

1907–21	E. H. Calloway
1922–24	Bonnell H. Stone
1925	Herbert L. Kayton
1926	M. T. Nichols
1927–28	C. B. Harman
1929–44	T. G. Woolford
1945	Hobart L. Manley
1946	R. H. White, Jr.
1947–49	W. Kirk Sutlive
1950–54	Hugh W. Dobbs
1955–56	Robert H. Rush
1957–58	W. M. Oettmeier, Sr.
1959–60	J. Frank Alexander
1961–62	Jim L. Gillis, Jr.
1963–64	Harley Langdale, Jr.
1965–66	George W. Peake, Jr.
1967–68	Edwin L. Douglass, Sr.
1969–70	Gerald B. Saunders
1971–72	Noll Van Cleave
1973–74	Shuford M. Wall
1975–76	Ben C. Meadows
1977–78	Edward W. Killorin
1979–80	W. J. "Bill" Barton
1981–82	Bobby J. Taylor
1983–84	Eley C. Frazer III
1984–85	W. F. "Bill" Torrey, Jr.

1985–86	Dr. Sydney B. Kinne III
1986–87	E. Owen Perry III
1987–88	William M. Oettmeier, Jr.
1988–89	C. Bonner Jones
1989–90	Larry S. Walker
1990–91	Dr. L. A. "Buddy" Hargreaves, Jr.
1991–92	William A. Binns
1992–93	Claude Yearwood
1993–94	H. Ed Hutcheson
1994–95	Sam P. Killian III
1995–96	Davis Dodge
1997	Alva Joe Hopkins III
1998	T. Gillis Morgan III
1999	Marshall Thomas
2000	William F. Miller III
2001	J. Blake Sullivan
2002	Paul Mott
2003	Miles Andy Stone
2004	Montgomery C. "Monty" Simpson
2005	David T. Foil

Wise Owl Award—GFA's Highest Award

1980	Edward W. Killorin
1981	Judge John A. Sibley
1982	A. Ray Shirley
1983	Sue Clark
1984	C. Bonner Jones
1985	Eley C. Frazer III
1986	Dean Leon A. "Buddy" Hargreaves
1987	James D. "Red" Strange
1988	William J. Barton
1989	Hugh M. Gillis, Sr.
1990	C. M. Stripling
1991	Larry Walker
1992	Dr. John E. Gunter
1993	Bill Dover
1994	Bill A. Binns
1995	Lewis Brown
1996	Harley Langdale, Jr.
1997	Fred W. Haeussler
1998	Bob Izlar
1999	Jim Fendig
2000	Joe Bennett
2001	William M. "Bill" Oettmeier, Jr.
2002	E. Owen Perry III
2003	Rusty Wood
2004	J. Blake Sullivan
2005	W. Earl Smith

1907–2007
GEORGIA
FORESTRY ASSOCIATION
WE GROW TREES

Tree Farmer of the Year

1968	Robert D. Humphrey
1969–72	———
1973	E. H. Armour
1974	———
1975	Jack Smith
1976	———
1977	Robert N. Leavell
1978	Winston Felder
1979	E. E. Gene Yawn
1980	Milton N. "Buddy" Hopkins, Jr.
	National & Southern Winner
1981	Wade Colquitt Hodges
1982	J. Merritt Abercrombie
1983	Grover Worsham
1984	Henry Owings
1985	Walter C. Merck
1986	C. M. Stripling
	National & Southern Winner
1987	Joe Bohannon
1988	Lamont Giddens
1989	Charles Parker
1990	Chuck and Rose Lane Leavell
1991	Frank A. Jordan, Jr.
1992	Lowry "Whitey" Hunt, Jr.
1993	Linda and Kirby Beam
1994	Dan Frailey
1995	Bill and Jean Lanier
1996	Dr. Hugh Hinely
1997	Roy Malone
	Southern Winner
1998	Chuck and Rose Lane Leavell
	National & Southern Winners
1999	Patricia McCarthy
2000	Laura and Don Devendorf
2001	Harley "Buck" Davis
2002	The Estes-Sherrill Family
2003	Banks Farm

| 2004 | Chesley Hilton |
| 2005 | Chuck and Beth Williams |

Logger of the Year

1986	Deck Trevitt
1987	Jim Evans
1988	Wade Payne
1989	Hill Logging, Inc.
1990	R. L. "Cotton" Boswell
1991	James J. Storey
1992	Shepherd Brothers Timber Company
1993	Wilson Brothers Logging

1994	W. C. Parker and Barnard Rahn
1995	John T. Lee
1996	Deck Trevitt
1997	Travis Reed
	National Winner 1998
1998	Bill Coleman
1999	Chris Weidner
2000	Jeff Alexander
2001	Scott Batson
2002	Allen Hawkins

GFA headquarters under construction and completed, 2003.
Courtesy GFA

2003	Bunn Logging
	National Winner 2004
2004	Murray Forestry
2005	Reece Logging

National Project Learning Tree Educator of the Year

1994	Chris Johnson
1996	Wanda Barrs
2000	Angie Davis
2002	Kris Irwin
2004	Jimmy Sanders

Georgia Forestry Association Staff 2006

Steve McWilliams	Executive Vice President
Judy Couch	Member Services Director
Alva Hopkins IV	Communications Director
Tim Lowrimore	Staff Forester
Carla Rapp	Forestry Education Director
Gini Seitz	Administrative Assistant
Telsa Stokes	Financial Administrator

Georgia Forestry Association Executive Staff

1907–14	Alfred A. Akerman, Secretary
1922–26 (?)	Bonnell H. Stone, Secretary
1954–68	Harvey R. Brown, Executive Director
1968–77	Harold Joiner, Executive Director
1977–86	H. Glenn Anthony, Executive Director
1987–98	Bob Izlar, Executive Director
1998–2000	Christopher Barneycastle, Executive Director
2000–01	Jim Doescher, Executive Director

Above left: Georgia Forestry Foundation Building, which serves as the headquarters of GFA, was formally occupied October 16, 2003. *Courtesy GFA*

Above right: Georgia Forestry Foundation Building lobby interior, 2004. *Courtesy GFA*

Left: Steve McWilliams, GFA Executive Vice President. *Courtesy GFA*

2001–02	E. Owen Perry III, Interim Executive Director
2002–03	Frank Montfort Riley, Jr., Interim Executive Director
2003–	Steve McWilliams, Executive Vice President

Georgia Forestry Foundation Trustees 2005

J. Blake Sullivan	Chairman
William F. Miller III	Vice Chairman
Marshall D. Thomas	Treasurer
Steve McWilliams	Secretary
David Foil	
Joe Hopkins III	
J. Wesley Langdale III	
Paul Mott	
Richard V. Saunders, Sr.	
Monte Simpson	
W. Earl Smith	
Miles Andy Stone	
Larry S. Walker	

Georgia Forestry Foundation, Inc.

The name of this foundation shall be the "Georgia Forestry Foundation, Inc.," hereinafter referred to as the "Foundation." The form of organization shall be that of a nonprofit corporation, incorporated under the laws of the State of Georgia.

The purposes and objectives of the foundation shall be:
1. To initiate, encourage and sponsor the development of technical and practical information of interest to the forestry community and the public in general and to publish or aid in the publication of this information.
2. To initiate, encourage and sponsor educational programs in forestry and other related subjects for private timberland owners and the public in general.
3. To advance instruction in forestry and encourage qualified individuals to enter careers in the field of forestry.
4. To initiate, encourage and sponsor research in forestry and effective teaching methods in forestry and publish or aid in the publication of the results of such research.
5. To advance a widespread knowledge of forestry among qualified students and the public in general.
6. To engage in related activities within the meaning of Section 501(c)(3) of the Internal Code or corresponding section of any future federal tax code.

Georgia Forestry Organizations

a p p e n d i x   f o u r

Georgia Forestry Commission Directors

Burley M. Lufburrow
1925–34

Elmer Dyal
1935–37

Frank Heyward, Jr.
1937–39

D. J. Weddell
1939

W. C. Hammerle
1939–41

Walter B. Dyal
1941–43

J. M. Tinker
1943–47

A. Ray Shirley
1947–49

Guyton Deloach
1949–60

A. Ray Shirley
1960–82

John W. Mixon
1983–95

David L. Westmoreland
1995–97

J. Frederick Allen
1997–2002

William R. Lazenby
(Interim) 2002–04

Kenneth C. Stewart, Jr.
2004–Present

GEORGIA FORESTRY COMMISSION

Georgia Forestry Commission headquarters, Dry Branch, Georgia, 2000.
Courtesy GFC

Courtesy TLC

American Turpentine Farmers Association

ATFA [first known as the American Turpentine Farmers Association Cooperative] was founded in 1934 in Valdosta, Georgia to promote the interests of turpentine farmers and producers. For many years, the Association was very active on behalf of its members. Judge Harley Langdale, Sr., Jim L. Gillis, Sr., Bill Oettmeier, Sr., Harley Langdale, Jr., and Jim L. Gillis, Jr., were leaders in ATF as well as other forestry interest groups. It sponsored the "Miss Gum Spirits of Turpentine" contest for Georgia's gum-producing counties for many years. ATFA is still in existence but has only a few members and meets briefly once a year. These industry standard rosin grades are provided by Harley Langdale, Jr.[1]

ATFA Rosin Grades

Light	Dark
X – Xtra white (lightest grade)	I – Isaac
WW – Water white	H – Harvey

Harley Langdale, Jr., demonstrating use of rosin grade paddle, 2000.
Courtesy TLC

WG – Window glass/ William	G – George
N – Nancy	F – Frank
M – Mary	B – Betsy
K – Kate	D – Dolly (darkest grade)

Southern Forest Institute

The Southern Forest Institute was formed in a 1969 merger of the Southern Pulpwood Conservation Association and the American Forest Institute southern region. It is now defunct.[2]

Society of American Foresters

Those who have served as president of SAF while resident in Georgia:

Charles F. Evans	President	1950–51
Ben Meadows	President	1972–73
Frederick Haeussler	President	1985
J. Walter Myers, Jr.	President	1987
William Barton	President	1991

Those who have served on SAF council while resident in Georgia:

Charles F. Evans	1946–47
G. D. Marckworth	1950–53
Henry J. Malsberger	1958–61, V.P.
B. E. Allen	1956–59
Archie E. Patterson	1962–65
Ben Meadows	1969
Frederick Haeussler	1983–84
Walt Myers	1987
William Barton	1991
Bob Lazenby	1997–99
Jim Doescher	2000–02

SAF President Ben Meadows, 1953. *Courtesy WSFNR*

SAF President Fred Haeussler, 2005. *Courtesy Sara Johnson*

SAF President Bill Barton. *Courtesy W. J. Barton*

SAF National Award Recipients

Barrington Moore Memorial Award

Claud L. Brown—1976
Donald H. Marx—1977

John A. Beale Memorial Award

Ben C. Meadows—1979
Fred W. Haeussler—1990

Professional Meritorious Service Award

Sid McKnight

Southeastern Society Georgia Division Fellows

Basil Ernie Allen	1964
George R. Barker	1985
William J. Barton	1987
Robert J. Beason	1986
Larry E. Biles	2001
Claud L. Brown	1979
Joe J. Brown	1988
William L. Consoletti, CF	2003
Douglass A. Craig	1979
Frank E. Craven	1987

Planting for the future. *Courtesy GFA*

Charles F. Evans	1949
James G. Fending, CF	2002
Eley C. Frazer III	1979
John E. Gunter	1990
Frederick W. Haeussler	1979
Sharon G. Haines	2003
Leon A. Hargreaves, Jr.	1981
Winfred N. Haynes	1986
Allyn Marsh Herrick	1977
Billy Humphries	2000
Robert L. Izlar, CF	2003
Charlie Bonner Jones	1984
Leroy Jones	1987
Louis F. Kalmar	1979
William E. Lancaster	2000
William R. Lazenby	1995
Arnett C. Mace, Jr.	1983
Barry F. Malac	1982
Henry J. Malsberger	1962
Gordon D. Marckworth	1955
Jack T. May	1979
Joseph S. McKnight	1971
Ben C. Meadows	1973
John W. Mixon	1990
J. Walter Myers, Jr.	1979
James E. Neal	1991
W. M. Oettmeier, Jr.	1994
Archie E. Patterson	1964
Charles B. Place, Jr.	2002
Paul H. Russell	1991
A. Ray Shirley	1979

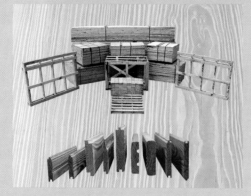

Top: Georgia framing lumber at work. *Courtesy GFA*

Bottom: An array of modern solid wood products. *Courtesy TLC*

J. D. "Red" Strange	1977
Klaus Steinbeck	1999
Earl L. Stone, Jr.	1968
Claude E. Yearwood	1992

Georgia Foresters Hall of Fame Recipients

1969	G. Norman Bishop
	Burley M. Lufburrow
	Charles Evans
	I. F. "Cap" Eldredge
	Bishop F. Grant
	Henry J. Malsberger
	William M. Oettmeier, Sr.
	Bonnell H. Stone
1970	Allyn M. Herrick
1971	Ernst V. Brender
	C. Dorsey Dyer
	J. D. "Red" Strange
1972	B. E. Allen
	A. C. Connaughton
	L. W. R. Jackson

1973	H. C. Carruth
	Ben C. Meadows
1974	Frank A. Bennett
	S. B. Kinne, Jr.
1975	H. Guyton DeLoach
1976	John W. Cooper
1977	William H. McComb
	Jack T. May
1978	Douglass A. Craig
1979	Archie E. Patterson
1980	James F. Spiers
	Robert W. Cooper
1981	William A. Campbell
	John F. Sisley
	Vernon Yow
1982	Leon A. Hargreaves, Jr.
	George A. Anderson
1983	John C. Barber
	Frederick W. Haeussler
	Charlie Bonner Jones
1984	Jerome L. Clutter
1985	Claud L. Brown
	"Ted" W. Earle, Sr.
	J. Walter Myers, Jr.

Medium-density fiberboard allows the use of smaller-diameter trees. *Courtesy TLC*

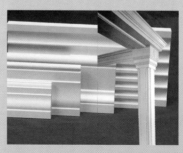

1986	H. Edward Ruark
1987	L. W. "Hoop" Eberhardt
1988	Harley Langdale, Jr.
	William Patrick Thomas
1989	None
1990	Barry F. Malac

1991	Joseph S. "Sid" McKnight
1992	W. M. "Bill" Oettmeier, Jr.
1993	None
1994	Eley C. Frazer III
1995	G. Edward Knapp
	Charles Fitzgerald
1996	None
1997	Robert L. Izlar
	John W. Mixon
1998	None
1999	William J. Barton
2000	A. Ray Shirley
2001	James G. Fendig
2002	James L. Gillis, Jr.
2003	William Eugene Lancaster
	Arnett C. Mace, Jr.
2004	John Reid Parker
2005	None

Forest Landowners Association

Landowner of the Year Award Georgia Recipients

1956	Governor Herman E. Talmadge
1966	U.S. Senator Richard B. Russell
1970	Judge Harley Langdale, Sr.
1971	Henry J. Malsberger
1973	T. W. Earle
1974	W. M. Oettmeier, Sr.
1983	J. Walter Myers, Jr.
1989	U.S. Representative Lindsay Thomas
1991	Harley Langdale, Jr.
1995	Eley C. Frazer III
1999	Honorable Williamson S. Stuckey, Jr.
2002	J. Blake Sullivan

Forest Landowner Association Georgia Presidents

1941–45, 1947–52	W. M. Oettmeier, Sr., Founder

1958–60	Harley Langdale, Jr.
1964–66	T. W. Earle, Sr.
1972–73	Lou F. Kalmar
1975–76	John F. Sisley
1979–80,	
1984–85	William M. Oettmeier, Jr.
1980–81	Noll A. Van Cleave
1983–84	Walter W. Herbst
1989–90	Eley C. Frazer III
1991–92	Dr. Sydney B. Kinne III
1993–94	Honorable Williamson S. Stuckey, Jr.
2005–07	Otis B. Ingram

Southern Forest World

Southern Forest World is a self-guided forestry museum located in Waycross. It was the idea of Sue Clark of Waycross, who nurtured the idea from concept to reality. Her plan was that there should be a museum dedicated to educating the public about the importance of forestry not just to Georgia but to the South. The Southern Forest World campus includes indoor exhibits and outdoor ones, including an original steam-powered logging locomotive.

Southern Forest World, Waycross, Georgia, 2005. *Courtesy Jimmy Herrin*

GOAL: Greater Okefenokee Association of Landowners

The Greater Okefenokee Association of Landowners was founded in 1994 by Okefenokee National Wildlife Refuge Manager Skippy Reeves; Bill Oettmeier, Jr., Superior Pine Products Company president; and Joe Hopkins III, Toledo Manufacturing Company president, to develop an effective firefighting partnership between federal, state, and private landowners in and around the Okefenokee Swamp. Today, the Florida Division of Forestry, Georgia Forestry Commission, and USDI Fish and Wildlife Service are cooperating members. In November 2005, GOAL received the U.S. Forest Service's coveted Edward Pulaski Award for excellence in firefighting, fire safety, and interagency cooperation.

Association of Consulting Foresters

The Association of Consulting Foresters of America, Inc. (ACF), was founded in 1948 to advance the professionalism, ethics, and interests of professional foresters whose primary work was consulting to the public. The ACF is the only national association for consulting foresters. Currently, there are more than 600 members in thirty-seven states and one Canadian province. The ACF is organized into state or multi-state chapters located in most forested regions of the U.S. There are twenty-two chapters, which hold regular meetings and pursue regional issues. A national office is maintained in the Washington, D.C., area to pursue national level issues and interact with other organizations involved in forest management. [From ACF website] The Georgia Chapter is quite active and holds yearly annual meetings around the state.

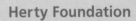

Herty Foundation

Herty is the oldest independent contractual research and development organization in the South. It was established by the Georgia Legislature in 1938 to recognize Dr. Charles H. Herty, who is considered the father of the southern U.S. paper and pulp industry. Herty is the only available site in the world that offers lab and pilot scale development and test market semi-production capability. The project managers and operators have produced sheets from literally hundreds of varieties of fiber blends. Herty offers services that many clients find unique—a maintenance staff that works with production operators to make rapid machinery changes to meet trial requirements, and a technical group that puts the client's needs first. [From Herty Foundation website] The governor appoints the

Top: Preserved logging train locomotive, Southern Forest World, Waycross, Georgia, 2005. *Courtesy Jimmy Herrin*

Bottom: GOAL Board members receiving U.S. Forest Service Pulaski Award for Fire Fighting Excellence. (L-R) George Constantino, Bill Oettmeier, Jr., Skippy Reeves, Mark Crowe, Jim Barrett, Wesley Langdale, Buck Wynn, Fargo, Georgia, 2005. *Courtesy Bill Oettmeier, Jr.*

Foundation's Board of Directors. The Herty Foundation was originally established by the Georgia General Assembly as the Savannah Pulp and Paper Laboratory in 1931.[3,4] In 1946 the General Assembly authorized the casting of a huge bronze plaque with a bust of Herty. It is displayed on the wall across from the Senate Chamber on the third floor of the state Capitol. Bas-reliefs of pines with Herty's famous cups and gutters and pulpmill smokestacks grace either side of the bust. The following inscription is at the top: "The spark of his genius and energy touched Georgia's pines, and forests of smokestacks began growing in the South."

Georgia State Board of Registration for Foresters

The Georgia State Board of Registration for Foresters was created by legislation enacted in 1951 for the purpose of protecting the public health, safety, and welfare by regulating those who engage in the practice of professional forestry. In order to carry out this charge, the Board has the authority to adopt rules, set standards for licensure, adopt mandatory standards of professional conduct, and investigate and discipline unauthorized, negligent or incompetent practice. The Board licenses registered foresters. Requirements for licensure as a registered forester include education, experience, and passage of an examination.

The Board is composed of six members appointed by the governor. Five members are registered foresters, and one member is appointed from the public at large. All members are appointed for terms of five years. The Board meets four times per year. Board members are: John W. Mixon, chairman; W. Dale Greene, vice chairman; James Frederick Allen; John Britt; Fred W. Greer, Jr.; and Charlie Bonner Jones. [From secretary of state's website]

USDA Forest Service Georgia Organization

District Rangers Tenure

Chattahoochee-Oconee National Forests

Armuchee Ranger District

Horace O. Mills	1939–41
Orrie W. Hanson	1941–43
Robert D. Williams	1943–52
Johnie E. Davis	1952–53
George W. Biskey	1953–57
William J. Chapparo	1957–60
John R. Allen	1960–63
John B. Fortin, Jr.	1963–66
Paul E. Fuller	1966–71
Jack R. McCormick	1971–73
R. Forrest Carpenter	1973–75
R. Paul Bullard	1975–82
Joe W. King	1982–2000

Armuchee Ranger District was consolidated with the Cohutta in 2001.

Armuchee/Cohutta Ranger District

Deborah Whitman	2001–Present

Brasstown Ranger District

Arthur W. Woody	1911–45
T. S. Seely	1945–51
Harry R. Wright	1951–58
S. F. Postlethwait	1958–61
Russell F. Griffith	1961–63
Lee E. Poague	1963–67
John B. Fortin, Jr.	1968–73
Jack R. McCormick	1973–81
Bobby Young	1981–90
Larry Luckett	1991–96
C. Dennis Daniel	1997–2000
R. Allen Polk	2000-Present

Georgia manufactured paper ready for shipment. *Courtesy GFA*

UGA Forestry Complex, ca. 2000s. *Courtesy WSFNR*

Chattooga Ranger District

Roscoe C. Nicholson	1936–51
W. O. Stewart	1951–53
George R. Anderson	1953–61
Ralph H. Freeman	1961–63
Lewis J. Smith	1963–74
Raymond T. Hawks	1974–98
Michael Grayson	1999–2005

Chestatee Ranger District

Del Edmundson	*
Arthur Woody	1918–45
Ted Sealy	1945–51
Spencer Palmer	1951–57
George W. Biskey	1957–71
George B. Hemingway	1971–75
Reese S. Scull	1975–78
Malcolm L. Jowers	1979–87
Art Bryant	1987–90
David P. Smith	1991–95

Chestatee District was consolidated with the Brasstown, Chattooga and Toccoa Districts in 1995.

*Note: At the beginning, the North Georgia area covering what is now Chestatee, Toccoa, and Brasstown was divided into three divisions, the Lower Toccoa, Three Forks, and Chestatee. Del Edmundson was head of the Lower Toccoa, but it cannot be determined if that was the Chestatee District, as it came to be known, or the Toccoa

District. The first ranger of the Chestatee District that incorporated the three divisions was Arthur Woody.

Cohutta Ranger District

Howard W. Burnett	1958–62
Berkeley J. Spilsbury	1962–65
Raymond G. Weidner	1965–72
Thomas O. Smith III	1973–78
William C. Black	1978–98
Alan Polk	1999–2000

Cohutta was combined with the Armuchee in 2001.

Tallulah Ranger District

R. C. Nicholson	1936–52
N. Bruce Alter	1952–61
Earl A. Parsons	1961–75
Forrest R. Carpenter	1975–78
Reese S. Scull	1978–88
David Jensen	1988–Present

Toccoa Ranger District

W. W. Bergoffen	1936–37
M. M. Bryan	1937–38
Joe J. Ennis	1938–42
Clinton G. Johnson	1942–43
G. E. Lethcoe	1943–47
Spencer H. Palmer	1947–51
Brooke R. Davis	1951–61
Stanley F. Postlethwait	1961–65
Henry F. Janssen	1965–68
Larry E. Cope	1968–74

W. A. Blalock	1974–79
Stephen F. Bailey	1980–97
Cassius Cash	2001–04

Oconee National Forest

Uncle Remus Ranger District

W. F. Leverett	From beginning of Land Utilization Project to 1950
B. G. Malone, Jr.	1961–76

Redlands Ranger District

B. D. Barr, Jr.	1961
Thomas W. Hardage	1961
Raymond G. Weidner	1962–65
Berkeley J. Spilsbury	1965–76

The Uncle Remus and Redlands Ranger Districts were consolidated into the Oconee Ranger District in October 1976.

Oconee Ranger District

B. G. Malone, Jr.	1976–77
John W. Moore	1977–94
Tony Tooke	1996–99
Barnie Gyant	2000–02
Bill Nightingale	2002–Present

Top: Barren cotton fields. Early Callaway Days, ca. early 1930s. *Courtesy Callaway Gardens and Rob Kindrick*

Bottom: From washed-out cotton land to productive forest, 2005. *Courtesy Callaway Gardens and Rob Kindrick*

Forest Supervisors

Chattahoochee–Oconee National Forests

	From	*Until*
P. F. Wallace Prater	July 1936	November 1936
William H. Fischer	December 1936	December 1940
Willis C. Branch	February 1941	July 1941
Hugh S. Redding	August 1941	September 1943
Clarence K. Spaulding	December 1943	August 1952
Fred N. Newnham	August 1952	March 1957
Paul Y. Vincent	March 1957	December 1965
Gilbert H. Stradt	February 1966	June 1967
Darold D. Westerberg	July 1967	August 1971
Vaughn H. Hofeldt	August 1971	March 1974
W. Pat Thomas	April 1974	December 1987
Kenneth D. Henderson	April 1988	August 1992
Kirby A. Brock	September 1992	February 1994
George G. Martin	February 1994	June 2000
Clara J. Johnson	November 2000	August 2002
Kathleen Atkinson	February 2003	Present

Southeastern Wood Producers Association

On February 3, 1990, a group of wood producers from Florida and Georgia met in Callahan, Florida, to form a nonprofit organization that would speak with a reasoned voice on their behalf and would give them an association dedicated strictly to their business.

The major goals of SWPA at the time of formation were: lower workers' compensation rates, affordable group insurance coverage, an effective legislative voice, responsible environmentalism, a positive public image, and timely news and economic data.

Charles Johns was the first president and led the organization for the first eight years. One of the organizers of the association and its first executive director was Clyde Barber, who was followed in this leadership position by Bill Nettles. Today the association is managed by Joe Allen.

The group has grown not only in numbers but in influence in Florida and Georgia, the entire South, and across the nation through its involvement with the American Loggers Council, of which it is a charter member.

SWPA's goal priority has changed considerably. SWPA is more concerned with legislative effectiveness, public image, and logger education offerings than ever before. SWPA leaders believe loggers can and should help control their destiny, not by disrupting business but by creating an effective organization to work within the system on their behalf.

—By Joe Allen

Opposite page: U.S. Forest Service foresters inspecting working compartment, ca. 1960s. *Courtesy WSFNR*

Ca. 2000. *Courtesy WSFNR*

Foreword

1. Forest History Society. 2005. *Stories of the forest: A campaign to put forest history to work.* Forest History Society pamphlet. Durham, NC, p. 2.

2. Leavell, Chuck. 2001. *Forever green: The history and hope of the American Forest.* Atlanta: Longstreet Press, p. 167.

Preface

1. Forest History Society. 2005. *Stories of the forest: A campaign to put forest history to work.* Forest History Society pamphlet. Durham, NC, p. i.

2. Ibid., p. 1–4.

3. University of Georgia yearbook.

4. May, Jack T. 1996. Letter to Dean Arnett C. Mace, Jr. December 12, p. 2.

Acknowledgments

1. Carlyle, Thomas. [1833] 2002. *Sartor resartus: The life and opinions of herr Teufelsdrockh.* LexisNexis: Gridiron Edition.

Introduction

1. Fitzgerald, Charlie. N.d. Typescript, p. 1.

2. Ibid., p. 1.

3. Ibid., p. 3.

Chapter One: 'Neath the Pine Trees' Stately Shadow

1. Wright, J. B., Jr. 1914. The University of Georgia alma mater, opening lines of second stanza.

2. American Forestry Association. 1926. *Forestry almanac: Semicentennial edition.* Philadelphia: J. B. Lippincott, p. 235–36.

3. Brown, R. Harold. 2002. *The greening of Georgia: The improvement of the environment in the twentieth century.* Macon: Mercer University Press, p. 24.

4. Plummer, Gayther L. 1975. 18th century forests in Georgia. *Bulletin of the Georgia Academy of Science.* 33:1.

5. Odum, Eugene P. and Turner, Monica G. 1990. The Georgia landscape: A changing resource. In *Changing landscapes: An ecological perspective.* New York: Springer-Verlag, p. 139.

6. Gerrell, Pete. 1999. *Old trees: The illustrated history of logging virgin timber in the southeastern U.S.* Crawfordville, FL: SYP Press, p. 5.

7. Plummer, Gayther L. 1975. 18th century forests in Georgia. *Bulletin of the Georgia Academy of Science.* 33:15.

8. Izlar, Wright. 1990. Interview by author. Waycross, GA. 5 October.

9. Stewart, Mart A. 2002. *"What nature suffers to groe": Life, labor, and landscape on the Georgia coast, 1680-1920.* Athens: University of Georgia Press, p. 214.

10. Reed, Thomas W. 1946. "George Foster Peabody School of Forestry." University of Georgia Library Reed Collection typescript. p. 2123.

11. Herty, Charles H. 1903. A new method of turpentine orcharding. USDA Bureau of Forestry Bulletin No. 40, p. 9.

12. Ibid., p. 42.

13. Carroll Butler's exhaustive, well illustrated book on working naval stores is a great source of material on the turpentine industry. Butler, Carroll B. 1998. *Treasures of the longleaf pines naval stores.* Shalimar, FL: Tarkel Publishing.

14. American Forestry Association. 1905. *Proceedings of the American forest congress.* Washington, D.C.: H. M. Suter Publishing Company, p. iii.

15. Ibid., p. 4.

16. Ibid., p. 35.

17. Berry College near Rome, GA, now holds that distinction.

18. American Forestry Association. 1905. *Proceedings of the American forest congress.* Washington, D.C.: H. M. Suter Publishing Company, p. 38.

19. Ibid., p. 39.

20. Clepper, Henry and Meyer, Arthur B. (eds.). 1960. *American forestry: Six decades of growth*. Washington, D.C.: Society of American Foresters, p. 5.

21. Reed, Thomas W. 1946. "George Foster Peabody school of forestry." University of Georgia Library Reed Collection typescript. p. 2123.

22. Ibid., p. 2124.

23. Holbrook, Alfred H. 1958. Peabody gifts. Typescript, p. 4.

24. Reed, Thomas W. 1946. "George Foster Peabody school of forestry." University of Georgia Library Reed Collection typescript. p. 2124.

25. Felty, Jr., Hilra H. 1970. A history of the school of forest resources, University of Georgia (1906–1969). Athens: School of Forest Resources Master of Forest Resources Problem, p. 38–39.

26. Reed, Thomas W. 1946. "George Foster Peabody school of forestry." University of Georgia Library Reed Collection typescript. p. 2124.

27. Ibid., p. 2125.

28. Ibid., p. 2126.

29. Ibid., p. 2128.

30. Reed, Thomas W. 1935. *David Crenshaw Barrow*. Athens: Published privately, p. 197.

31. Marckworth, Gordon D. 1932. A history of the Georgia forest school. *Cypress Knee* 10:54.

32. Reed, Thomas W. 1946. "George Foster Peabody school of forestry." University of Georgia Library Reed Collection typescript. p. 2127.

33. Akerman, Alfred. 1906. Third annual report of the state forester. Commonwealth of Massachusetts. House No. 200, p. 19.

34. The title "chancellor" was used to describe the heads of the different college-level institutions in Georgia before the Reorganization Act of 1931. After that, the chancellor was the head of the University System of Georgia, and institutional heads became "presidents."

35. Barrow, D. C. 1916. Chancellor of the University of Georgia in "What people think." *Forest Club Annual*. 1:8.

Chapter Two: Influence for a Proper Understanding

1. Marckworth, Gordon D. 1932. A history of the Georgia Forest School. *Cypress Knee* 10:55. From part of the University of Georgia Department of Forestry Inaugural Address delivered by Alfred Gaskill, USFS, on November 27, 1906.

2. While the Trustees accepted Peabody's gift and voted to establish the George Foster Peabody School of Forestry, for some reason it was dedicated as a Department of Forestry.

3. Reed, Thomas W. 1946. "George Foster Peabody School of Forestry." University of Georgia Library Reed Collection typescript. p. 2128.

4. Marckworth, Gordon D. 1932. A history of the Georgia Forest School. *Cypress Knee*. 10:55.

5. Bruncken, Ernest. 1900. *North American forests and forestry: Their relations to the national life of the American people*. New York: G. P. Putnam's Sons, p. 248.

6. Georgia Forestry Commission. 1956. From then…'Til now: History of Peabody Forestry School. *Georgia Forestry*. 9, no. 9:2.

7. Reed, Thomas W. 1946. "George Foster Peabody School of Forestry." University of Georgia Library Reed Collection typescript. p. 2124.

8. Ibid. 1946. "George Foster Peabody School of Forestry." University of Georgia Library Reed Collection typescript. p. 2127.

9. Mathis, Ray (ed.). 1974. *"Uncle Tom" Reed's memoir of the University of Georgia*. Athens: University of Georgia Libraries Miscellanea Publications No. 11, p. 25.

10. Akerman, Alfred A. 1907. Annual report to the chancellor and faculty. May 23. Manuscript.

11. Idem. 1908. 1907–1908 Forestry statement of expenses. Manuscript. p. 1.

12. Idem. 1909. 1908–1909 Annual report. Manuscript. 6p.

13. Soule, Andrew M. 1930. A brief history of the Division of Forestry. *Cypress Knee*. 8:36.

14. Akerman, Alfred A. 1911. Annual report of the School of Forestry to the chancellor and faculty. Manuscript. 2p.

15. Idem. 1912. 1911–1912 State College of Agriculture and Mechanic Arts annual report to Dean Andrew M. Soule. Manuscript. 1p.

16. Idem. 1914. Report to the chancellor and faculty. Manuscript. 2p.

17. Marckworth, Gordon D. 1932. A history of the Georgia Forest School. *Cypress Knee.* 10:56.

18. School of Forest Resources. 1981. Seventy-five years service. University of Georgia School of Forest Resources. Duplicated, p. 3.

19. Felty, Jr., Hilra H. 1970. A history of the School of Forest Resources, University of Georgia (1906–1969). Athens: School of Forest Resources Master of Forest Resources Problem, p. 7.

20. Karina, Stephen J. 1987. *The University of Georgia College of Agriculture: An administrative history, 1785–1985.* Athens: University of Georgia College of Agriculture, p. 131.

21. Ibid., p. 139.

22. Soule, Andrew M. 1928. Our forest nursery. *Cypress Knee.* 6:9.

23. School of Forest Resources. 1981. Seventy-five years service. University of Georgia School of Forest Resources. Duplicated, p. 3.

24. Darby, Sanford. 1967. Fifty years of seedling production in Georgia. *TOPS.* 1, no. 3:14.

25. Marckworth, Gordon D. 1932. A history of the Georgia Forest School. *Cypress Knee.* 10:78.

26. Bishop, G. N. and B. F. Grant. 1957. Golden anniversary: Our first fifty years. *Cypress Knee.* 33:105.

27. Trowbridge, K. S. 1929. Georgia Forest School shows progress. *Cypress Knee.* 7:35.

28. Felty, Jr., Hilra H. 1970. A history of the School of Forest Resources, University of Georgia (1906–1969). Athens: School of Forest Resources Master of Forest Resources Problem, p. 12.

29. Doherty, C. P. 1926. Our cabin. *Cypress Knee.* 4:8–10.

30. Allen, Richard C. 1937. History of the forestry cabin. *Cypress Knee.* 15:36. Dick Allen had a distinguished international career with Weyerhaeuser Company and was Mississippi state forester in the 1980s.

31. Burleigh, Thomas D. 1923. The Division of Forestry. *The Forest Club Annual.* 1:8.

32. Roper, Daniel M. 1996. Watson Springs Resort. *North Georgia Journal.* 13, no. 1: 8–11.

33. Rosser, E. J. 1923. The logging engineers take a trip to the swamps. *The Forestry Club Annual.* 1:9–16.

34. Kollock, J. T. 1932. Through the years with the alumni. *Cypress Knee.* 10:57.

35. School of Forest Resources. 1968. News release announcing name change for the school. University of Georgia School of Forest Resources. Duplicated, p. 5.

36. American Tree Association. 1926. *Forestry almanac: Semicentennial edition.* Philadelphia: J. B. Lippincott, p. 200–201.

37. Soule, Andrew M. 1930. A brief history of the division of forestry. *Cypress Knee.* 8:36.

38. Ibid., p. 38.

39. Ibid., p. 38.

40. Trowbridge, K. S. 1929. Georgia Forest School shows progress. *Cypress Knee.* 7:38.

41. School of Forest Resources. 1968. News release announcing name change for the school. University of Georgia School of Forest Resources. Duplicated, p. 5.

42. Bishop, G. N. and B. F. Grant. 1957. Golden anniversary: Our first fifty years. *Cypress Knee.* 33:104.

43. School of Forest Resources. 1968. News release announcing name change for the school. University of Georgia School of Forest Resources. Duplicated, p. 5.

44. Brooks, Robert P. 1956. *The University of Georgia under sixteen administrations: 1788–1955.* Athens: University of Georgia Press, p. 134.

45. Graves, Henry S. 1930. Trends in forestry education. *Cypress Knee.* 8:49.

46. Chapman, H. H. 1935. *Professional forestry schools report: Giving the comparative status of those institutions that offered instruction in professional forestry for the school year 1934–35.* Washington, D.C.: Society of American Foresters, p. xiii.

47. Langdale, Harley, Jr. 2005. Interview by author. Valdosta, GA. 7 September.

48. Ibid.

49. Pikl, I. James, Jr. 1966. *A history of Georgia forestry*. Athens: University of Georgia Bureau of Business and Economic Research, Research Monograph No. 2, p. 32.

50. Student Body, The. 1937. Do you know? 4p.

51. Langdale, Harley, Jr. 2005. Interview by author. Valdosta, GA. 7 September.

52. Ibid.

53. *Southern Lumberman*. 1939. Georgia Forestry School paneled in native woods. January 15.

54. George Foster Peabody School of Forestry. 1939. Program for the presentation of the bust of George Foster Peabody. April 27. George Foster Peabody School of Forestry. Duplicated.

55. Georgia Forestry Commission. 1956. Students encouraged in campus activities. *Georgia Forestry*. 9, no. 9:8.

56. Weddell, D. J. 1943. Your School of Forestry. *Cypress Knee*. 21:13.

57. Idem. 1946. The war years at the school. *Cypress Knee*. 22:17.

58. Dyer, Thomas G. 1985. *The University of Georgia: A bicentennial history, 1785–1985*. Athens: University of Georgia Press, p. 242.

59. School of Forest Resources. 1968. News release announcing name change for the school. University of Georgia School of Forest Resources. Duplicated, p. 7.

60. Ibid., p. 8.

61. Sizemore, William R. 1964. A model procedure for estimating fair market value of southern forest lands with special reference to eminent domain proceedings. Ph.D. diss., University of Georgia.

62. School of Forest Resources. 1968. News release announcing name change for the school. University of Georgia School of Forest Resources. Duplicated, p. 1.

63. Cowdrey, Albert E. 1983. *This land, this south: An environmental history*. Lexington: University of Kentucky Press, p. 137.

64. Association of Southern Forestry Clubs. 1969. *The Southern Forester*, p. 18.

65. Idem. 1982. *The Southern Forester*, p. 7.

66. School of Forestry. 1950. A forest research program for Georgia. University of Georgia School of Forestry. Duplicated, p. 3.

67. Ibid., p. 5–9.

68. Hargreaves, L. A., Jr., and Campbell, W. A. 1979. School of Forest Resources research for the 1980's. University of Georgia School of Forest Resources. Duplicated, p. 3.

69. Ibid., p. 16.

70. Ibid., p. 26.

71. U.S. Department of Agriculture Forest Service. 1979. History of cooperation between the School of Forest Resources and the U.S. Department of Agriculture through the Division of Forest Pathology and the Forest Service. USDA Forest Service. Duplicated, p. 2.

72. Ibid., p. 2.

73. Hargreaves, L. A., Jr. 1982. Forestry education—Prospects for the future. *TOPS*. 15, no. 1:18–19.

74. Haynes, W. N. 1982. Forest business management at the School of Forest Resources, University of Georgia. *TOPS*. 15, no. 3:12–13.

75. Izlar, Bob. 1984. University of Georgia Center for Forest Business Management. American Pulpwood Association Technical Release 84-R-14, Washington, D.C., 2p.

76. Campbell, W. Andy. 1978. The School of Forest Resources: University of Georgia. University of Georgia School of Forest Resources. Duplicated, p. 2–3.

77. Haynes, W. N. 1991. Daniel B. Warnell. *TOPS*. 23, no. 2:14.

78. Industrial Department Seaboard Air Line Railroad Company. 1956. Golden anniversary: George Foster Peabody School of Forestry. *Forestry Bulletin*. 46:n.p.

79. Georgia Forestry Commission. 1956. 50 years of progress. *Georgia Forestry*. 9, no. 9:1.

80. Ibid., p. 1.

81. School of Forest Resources. 1981. Seventy-five years service. University of Georgia School of Forest Resources. Duplicated, p. 9–10. Paraphrased to update.

Chapter Three: A Need for Advocacy

1. Walker, Laurence C. 1991. *The southern forest: A chronicle.* Austin: University of Texas Press, p. 187.

2. Reed, Thomas W. 1946. "George Foster Peabody School of Forestry." University of Georgia Library Reed Collection typescript. p. 2127.

3. Myers, J. Walter, Jr. 1988. *Impact of forestry associations on productivity in the south's forests.* U.S. Department of Agriculture Forest Service, Miscellaneous Publication No. 1458, p. 28.

4. Akerman, Alfred. 1907. Annual report to the chancellor and faculty. May 23. Manuscript.

5. Brown, Leon. 1982. 75 years of GFA—An anniversary special. *TOPS.* 15, no. 2:26.

6. Ibid., p. 26.

7. Kinney, J. P. [1917] 1972. *The development of forest law in America.* Reprint, New York: Arno Press, p. 24.

8. Ibid., p. 26.

9. American Tree Association. 1926. *Forestry almanac: Semicentennial edition.* Philadelphia: J. B. Lippincott, p. 236.

10. Bruncken, Ernest. 1900. *North American forests and forestry: Their relations to the national life of the American people.* New York: G. P. Putnam's Sons, p. 209.

11. Duerr, William A. (ed.). 1973. *Timber! Problems, prospects, policies.* Ames: Iowa State University Press, p. 168.

12. Harman, C. B. 1926. Our forests today and twenty years hence. *Cypress Knee.* 4:11.

13. Garrison, P. M. 1929. Practicing industrial forestry in southern pine. *Cypress Knee.* 7:63.

14. Fickle, James E. 1980. *The new south and the "new competition": Trade association development in the southern pine industry.* Urbana: University of Illinois Press, p. 19.

15. Ibid., p. 60–61.

16. Langdale, Harley, Jr. 1991. As I remember it. *Forest Farmer.* 50, no. 6:7.

17. Myers, J. Walter, Jr. 1988. *Impact of forestry associations on productivity in the south's forests.* U.S. Department of Agriculture Forest Service, Miscellaneous Publication No. 1458, p. 28.

18. Brown, Leon. 1982. Jim L. Gillis, Jr.: GFA president 1961–1962. *TOPS.* 15, no. 2:11.

19. Langdale, Harley, Jr. 2005. Interview by author. Valdosta, GA. 7 September.

20. Outland III, Robert B. 2004. *Tapping the pines: The naval stores industry in the American south.* Baton Rouge: Louisiana State University Press, p. 225.

21. Langdale, Harley, Jr. 2005. Interview by author. Valdosta, GA. 7 September.

22. Norton, Eliot. 1923. The interest of banks and trust companies in forestry. *Cypress Knee.* 1:28-31.

23. Langdale, Harley, Jr. 2005. Interview by author. Valdosta, GA. 7 September.

24. Duerr, William A. (ed.). 1973. *Timber! Problems, prospects, policies.* Ames: Iowa State University Press, p. 169.

25. Barrett, DuPre. 1930. A business view of the cut over lands of the south. *Cypress Knee.* 8:44.

26. Stone, Bonnell H. 1923. The Georgia For[e]stry Association. *The Forestry Club Annual.* 1:23, 28–30.

27. Georgia Forestry Association. 1933. Articles of association: Georgia Forestry Association by-laws and constitution. Duplicated, p. 1.

28. Brown, Leon. 1982. 75 years of GFA—An anniversary special. *TOPS.* 15, no. 2:27.

29. Hargreaves, L. A., Jr. 1953. The Georgia Forestry Commission—objectives, organization, policies and procedures. Ph.D. diss., University of Michigan, p. 13–14.

30. Ibid., p. 16.

31. Allen, William F. 1981. Herty Foundation history. Herty Foundation. Duplicated.

32. Herty, Charles Holmes. 1937. The pulp and paper laboratory at Savannah: Its history, operation and future. Savannah Pulp and Paper Laboratory. Duplicated.

33. Hargreaves, L. A., Jr. 1953. The Georgia Forestry Commission—objectives, organization, policies and procedures. Ph.D. diss., University of Michigan, p. 16.

34. Chapman, H. H. 1936. Letter to Governor Eugene Talmadge of Georgia. *Journal of Forestry.* 34, no. 4:431.

35. Talmadge, Eugene. 1936. Letter to H. H. Chapman. *Journal of Forestry.* 34, no. 4:432.

36. Chapman, H. H. 1936. Letter of reply to Governor Eugene Talmadge of Georgia. *Journal of Forestry.* 34, no. 4:432.

37. Hargreaves, L. A., Jr. 1953. The Georgia Forestry Commission—objectives, organization, policies and procedures. Ph.D. diss., University of Michigan, 18.

38. Ibid., p. 19.

39. Ibid., p. 19.

40. Ibid., p. 22.

41. Talmadge, Herman E. and Winchell, Mark Royden. 1987. *Talmadge—A political legacy, a political life: A memoir*. Atlanta: Peachtree Publishers, p. 111.

42. Ibid., p. 110.

43. Ibid., p. 110–11.

44. State Department of Forestry. 1926. *First biennial report of the State Department of Forestry to the governor and General Assembly of the state of Georgia: 1925–1926*. Atlanta, p. 13.

45. Ibid., p. 10.

46. Ibid., p. 14.

47. Ibid., p. 12.

48. Ibid., p. 27.

49. Ibid., p. 33.

50. Ibid., p. 21.

51. Ibid., p. 22.

52. McClelland, W. Craig. 1995. *Union Camp Corporation: A legacy of leadership*. The Newcomen Society of the United States, Newcomen Publication No. 1453, p. 17.

53. Clepper, Henry. 1971. *Professional forestry in the United States*. Baltimore: The Johns Hopkins Press, p. 251.

54. Brown, Leon. 1982. 75 years of GFA—An anniversary special. *TOPS*. 15, no. 2:28.

55. Hodgson, Richard S. 1970. *In quiet ways—George H. Mead: The man and the company*. Dayton: The Mead Corporation, p. 224.

56. Ibid., p. 192.

57. Ibid., p. 192–93.

58. Boerker, Richard H. D. 1945. *Behold our green mansions: A book about American forests*. Chapel Hill: University of North Carolina Press, p. 226.

59. Hopkins, Milton N., Jr. 2001. *In one place: The natural history of a Georgia farmer*. St. Simons Island, GA: The Saltmarsh Press.

60. Agricultural Extension Service. 1950. *Georgia agricultural handbook*. Athens: University System of Georgia, p. 281.

61. Plummer, Gayther L. 1976. Mulberries to soybeans: Changing vegetation patterns. *Bulletin of the Georgia Academy of Science*. 34:185.

62. Idem. 1975. 18th century forests in Georgia. *Bulletin of the Georgia Academy of Science*. 33:1.

63. Odum, Eugene P. and Turner, Monica G. 1990. The Georgia landscape: A changing resource. In *Changing landscapes: An ecological perspective*. New York: Springer-Verlag, p. 137.

64. Clark, Thomas D. 1984. *The greening of the south: The recovery of land and forest*. Lexington: University of Kentucky Press, p. 146.

65. International Paper Company. 1997. *A history of southlands experiment forest*. New York: International Paper Company, p. ix.

66. Ibid., p. 3.

67. Clepper, Henry. 1971. *Professional forestry in the United States*. Baltimore: The Johns Hopkins Press, p. 92.

68. U.S. Department of Agriculture Agricultural Marketing Service. 1957. *Georgia agricultural facts 1900–1956*. Georgia Agricultural Extension Service Bulletin 511 (revised). Athens, p. 205.

69. Union Bag Camp Paper Corporation. 1959. Nursery announcement. Typescript.

70. Union Bag-Camp Athletic Association. 1960. In the ground and growing—quite a feat: 100,000, 000 trees. *The Digester*. 25, no. 3:5.

71. Brown, Leon. 1982. 75 years of GFA—An anniversary special. *TOPS*. 15, no. 2:28.

72. Idem. 1982. W. Kirk Sutlive: GFA past president 1947–1949. *TOPS*. 15, no. 1:13.

73. Rossoll, Harry. 1968. Why symbols? *TOPS*. 2, no. 4:6.

74. Shirley, A. Ray. 1967. Georgia's changing land patterns. *TOPS.* 2, no. 1:42–43.

75. McCaffrey, J. E. 1967. Georgia forestry's changing times 1907–1937. *TOPS.* 2, no. 1:5, 28–29, 33.

76. McSwiney, E. V. 1967. Georgia forestry's changing times 1937–1967. *TOPS.* 2, no. 1:15, 21, 24.

77. Duncan, Jr., John P. 1967. Georgia forestry's changing times 1967–1997. *TOPS.* 2, no. 1:32, 36.

78. Sutton, V. J. 1968. "Twenty years of green." *TOPS.* 3, no. 1:4, 30.

79. [Georgia Forestry Association]. 1968. Forest industry safety inspections. *TOPS.* 2, no. 3:4.

80. Idem. 1982. GFA gives first woods arson awards. *TOPS.* 15, no. 1:26.

81. Bennett, Howard. 1990. 50 years of Miss Georgia Forestry. *TOPS.* 24, no. 2:39–40.

82. Izlar, Bob. 1990. General Assembly sets stage for landmark ad valorem tax reform. *TOPS.* 24, no. 1:8.

83. Idem. 1990. Conservation use amendment will keep Georgia green and growing. *TOPS.* 24, no. 3:7.

84. Underwood, Rudy and Ray, Bob. 1990. Status of property tax-related legislation. *TOPS.* 24, no. 2:20.

85. Izlar, Bob. 1990. Conservation use amendment will keep Georgia green and growing. *TOPS.* 24, no. 3:6–7.

86. Tankersley, Larry A., Gunter, John E. and Dangerfield, Coleman W., Jr. 1990. House Resolution 836, proposed ad valorem tax changes. *TOPS.* 24, no. 3:9. It turned out to be just as they predicted.

87. Stripling, C. M. 1990. Why I'm for the conservation use amendment: Question #3. *TOPS.* 24, no. 3:10–11.

88. Izlar, Bob. 1991. One year after Amendment Three: Where are we? *TOPS.* 25, no. 4:6–7, 9.

89. Idem. 1991. Conservation use legislation: Update II. *TOPS.* 25, no. 3:6.

90. Idem. 1991. Conservation use legislation—summary. *TOPS.* 25, no. 1:14–15.

91. Idem. 1995. Farm, forestry and environmental groups agree. *TOPS.* 29, no. 1:33.

92. Clark, Anna. 1997. Volunteers set world record on tree-rific Arbor Day. *Macon Telegraph.* February 22, A1.

Chapter Four: A Common Future

1. Clepper, Henry. 1971. *Professional forestry in the United States.* Baltimore: The Johns Hopkins Press, p. 235–36.

2. Myers, J. Walter, Jr. 1988. *Impact of forestry associations on productivity in the south's forests.* U.S. Department of Agriculture Forest Service, Miscellaneous Publication No. 1458, p. 28.

3. Brown, Leon. 1982. Harley Langdale, Jr.: GFA president 1963–1964. *TOPS.* 15, no. 3:9.

4. Healy, Robert G. 1985. *Competition for land in the American south.* Washington, D.C.: The Conservation Foundation, p. 276.

5. MacCleery, Douglas W. 1992. *American forests: A history of resiliency and recovery.* U.S. Department of Agriculture Forest Services, FS-540, p. 55.

6. Ibid., p. 56.

7. Ibid., p. 56.

8. Paraphrase of a statement generally attributed to Dr. Rupert Cutler.

Appendix One: Champions of Forestry

Author's note: Rather than clutter the profile of each person with footnotes, I have chosen to list here the references consulted for each champion.

George Foster Peabody

1. School of Forest Resources. 1981. Seventy-five years service. University of Georgia School of Forest Resources. Duplicated, p. 1.

2. Holbrook, Alfred H. 1958. Peabody gifts. Typescript. 4p.

3. Reed, Thomas W. 1946. "George Foster Peabody School of Forestry." University of Georgia Library Reed Collection typescript. P. 2123.

4. George Foster Peabody School of Forestry. 1939. Program for the presentation of the bust of George Foster Peabody. April 27. George Foster Peabody School of Forestry. Duplicated, p. 2.

Charles Holmes Herty

1. Reed, Germaine M. 1995. *Crusading for chemistry: The professional career of Charles Holmes Herty.* Athens: University of Georgia Press, p. 4.

2. Cameron, Frank K. 1939. Charles Holmes Herty. *Journal of the American Chemical Society.* 61:1619.

3. Mathis, Ray (ed.). 1974. *"Uncle Tom" Reed's memoir of the University of Georgia.* Athens: University of Georgia Libraries Miscellanea Publications No. 11, p. 141–42.

4. Stegeman, John F. 1966. *The ghosts of Herty Field: Early days on a southern gridiron.* Athens: University of Georgia Press, p. 2.

5. Whitehead, T. H. 1976. Georgia's nineteenth century chemists. *Bulletin of the Georgia Academy of Science.* 34:202.

6. Cowdrey, Albert E. 1983. *This land, this south: An environmental history.* Lexington: University of Kentucky Press, p. 137.

7. Reed, Gerry. 1982. Saving the naval stores industry: Charles Holmes Herty's cup-and-gutter experiments 1900–1905. *Journal of Forest History.* 26:173.

8. Earley, Lawrence S. 2004. *Looking for longleaf: The fall and rise of an American forest.* Chapel Hill: University of North Carolina Press, p. 147.

9. Herty, Charles Holmes. 1937. The pulp and paper laboratory at Savannah: Its history, operation and future. Savannah Pulp and Paper Laboratory. Duplicated, p. 1.

10. Allen, William F. 1981. Herty Foundation history. Herty Foundation. Duplicated, p. 3.

11. Bates, William M. 1967. James Fowler—Pioneer tree planter. *TOPS.* 2, no. 3:15.

12. Herty, Charles H. 1929. The future of cellulose. *Cypress Knee.* 7:60-62.

Alfred A. Akerman

1. Walker, Laurence C. 1991. *The southern forest: A chronicle.* Austin: University of Texas Press, p. 187.

2. Kollock, J. T. 1932. Through the years with the alumni. *Cypress Knee.* 10:57.

Jim L. Gillis, Sr.

1. American Tree Association. 1924. *Forestry almanac.* Philadelphia: J. P. Lippincott, p. 72.

2. Gerrell, Pete. 1998. *The illustrated history of the naval stores (turpentine) industry with artifact guide, home remedies, recipes and jokes.* Crawfordville, FL: SYP Press, p. 12.

William M. Oettmeier, Sr.

1. *Superior Pine Products Co. v. United States.* 201 Ct. Cl. 73 1 U.S.T.C. ¶9348; 31 AFTR 2d 1134 (1973), p. 9.

2. Oettmeier, William M. Jr. 1991. Why? *Forest Farmer.* 50, no. 6:10.

3. Amigo, Eleanor and Neuffer, Mark. 1980. *Beyond the Adirondacks: The story of St. Regis Paper Company.* Westport, CN: Greenwood Press, p. 101.

4. Eldridge, I. M. 1929. Suwannee forest. *Cypress Knee.* 7:66–68.

5. Langdale, Harley, Jr. 1991. As I remember it. *Forest Farmer.* 50, no. 6:6.

6. Oettmeier, W. M. 1933. Forestry in southeast Georgia. *Cypress Knee.* 11:39–41.

7. [Georgia Forestry Association]. 1968. Meet William M. Oettmeier—Longtime G. F. A. member. *TOPS.* 2, no. 4:10.

Harley Langdale, Jr.

1. Lancaster, John E. 2002. *Judge Harley and his boys: The Langdale story.* Macon: Mercer University Press.

2. Langdale, Harley, Jr. 1991. As I remember it. *Forest Farmer.* 50, no. 6:6–9.

3. Idem. 2005. Interview by author. Valdosta, GA. 7 September.

4. [Warren, B. Jack]. 1991. Forest farmers association through the years. *Forest Farmer.* 50, no. 6:18.

Archie Edgar Patterson

1. Patterson, Archie E. 1994. Ethics in forestry: Four self-help questions. In *Ethics in forestry,* edited by Lloyd C. Irland. Portland, OR: Timber Press, p. 45–47.

Appendix Two: Warnell School of Forestry and Natural Resources

1. Jayhole Club, University of Georgia Chapter. 1976. Constitution and bylaws. University of Georgia School of Forest Resources. Duplicated, p. 1.

2. Izlar, Bob. 1991. Jayhole legend. Jayhole Club, University of Georgia Chapter. Duplicated.

3. AGHON Society. 1920. AGHON charter. AGHON Society, University of Georgia.

4. Forest Club of the University of Georgia, The. 1914–1923. Minutes of the Forest Club. School of Forestry, University of Georgia, p. 5.

5. Ibid., p. 7.

6. Ibid., p. 11.

7. Ibid., p. 13.

8. Ibid., p. 21.

9. Ibid., p. 29.

10. Ibid., p. 41.

11. Ibid., p. 45.

12. Ibid., p. 49.

13. Ibid., p. 57.

14. *Forest Club Annual*. 1917. 1, p. 7.

15. Thurmond, A. K., Jr. 1928. Cypress Knees. *Cypress Knee*. 6:49.

16. Idem. 1928. Our club. *Cypress Knee*. 6:7.

17. Brown, E. O. 1939. The senior camp log. University of Georgia George Foster Peabody School of Forestry. Duplicated.

18. Blalock, Tommy. 1959. Georgia's summer foresters learn by doing. *Georgia Agriculturalist*. 51, no. 1:8–10.

19. Thurmond, A. K., Jr. 1928. Our club. *Cypress Knee*. 6:7.

20. Grant, B. F. 1925. Activities of the forestry club. *Cypress Knee*. 7:16.

21. Society of Xi Sigma Pi, The National Forestry Honor Society. 2005. *Newsletter*. 36:1.

22. Information provided by Drs. Karl Miller and Bryan Chapman.

23. Information provided by Dr. Todd Rasmussen.

24. Flinchum, D. M. 1971. Criteria for the design of recreation areas on flood plains of the north Georgia piedmont. Master's thesis, University of Georgia.

25. Van Den Avyle, M. J. 1983. History of the Georgia Cooperative Fishery Research Unit. Georgia Cooperative Fish and Wildlife Unit. Duplicated.

26. Information provided by Dr. Cecil Jennings.

27. *Savannah Morning News*. 2005. Obituary of Burley Brown Lufburrow, 9 June.

28. University of Georgia Hargrett Rare Book Room Forestry Estrays Collection.

Appendix Four: Georgia Forestry Organizations

1. Langdale, Harley, Jr. 2005. Interview by author. Valdosta, GA. 7 September.

2. Georgia Forestry Association. 1969. Merger creates new forest institute. *TOPS*. 3, no. 3:20.

3. Allen, William F. 1981. Herty Foundation history. Herty Foundation. Duplicated, p. 1.

4. Herty, Charles H. 1937. The pulp and paper laboratory at Savannah: Its history, operation and future. Savannah Pulp and Paper Laboratory. Duplicated, p. 1.

About the Author

1. The literal translation from the vulgate Latin is "Consider those canines," but Georgia Bulldogs know it best as "How 'Bout Them Dawgs!"

Abbreviations

AFF	American Forest Foundation
ATFA	American Turpentine Farmers Association
ATFS	American Tree Farm System
CN	*Cypress Knee*, annual publication of the Forestry Club (1923–72)
FLA	Forest Landowners Association (formerly Forest Farmers Association)
GFA	Georgia Forestry Association, Inc.
GFC	Georgia Forestry Commission
GFF	Georgia Forestry Foundation
GFRC	Georgia Forest Research Council
G-P	Georgia-Pacific Corporation
IP	International Paper Company
PLT	Project Learning Tree
SAF	Society of American Foresters
SESAF	Southeastern Section Society of American Foresters
SWPA	Southeastern Wood Producers Association
TLC	The Langdale Company
TOPS	Georgia Forestry Association magazine
UCC	Union Camp Corporation
UGA	University of Georgia
USFS	U.S. Forest Service
USDA	U.S. Department of Agriculture
WSFNR	Warnell School of Forestry and Natural Resources

Literature Cited

Akerman, Alfred. 1906. Third annual report of the state forester. Commonwealth of Massachusetts. House No. 200.

_____. 1907. Annual report to the chancellor and faculty. May 23. Manuscript.

_____. 1908. 1907–1908 Forestry statement of expenses. Manuscript. 1p.

_____. 1909. 1908–1909 Annual report. Manuscript. 6p.

_____. 1911. Annual report of the School of Forestry to the chancellor and faculty. Manuscript. 2p.

_____. 1912. 1911–1912 State College of Agriculture and Mechanic Arts annual report to Dean Andrew M. Soule. Manuscript. 1p.

_____. 1914. Report to the chancellor and faculty. Manuscript. 2p.

AGHON Society. 1920. AGHON charter. AGHON Society, University of Georgia.

Agricultural Extension Service. 1950. *Georgia agricultural handbook.* Athens: University System of Georgia.

Allen, Richard C. 1937. History of the forestry cabin. *Cypress Knee.* 15: 36.

Allen, William F. 1981. Herty Foundation history. Herty Foundation. Duplicated.

American Forestry Association. 1905. *Proceedings of the American Forest Congress.* Washington, D.C.: H. M. Suter Publishing Company.

American Tree Association. 1924. *Forestry almanac.* Philadelphia: J. P. Lippincott.

_____. 1926. *Forestry almanac: Semicentennial edition.* Philadelphia: J. B. Lippincott.

Amigo, Eleanor and Neuffer, Mark. 1980. *Beyond the Adirondacks: The story of St. Regis Paper Company.* Westport, CT: Greenwood Press.

Association of Southern Forestry Clubs. 1969. *The Southern Forester.*

_____. 1976. *The Southern Forester.*

_____. 1982. *The Southern Forester.*

_____. 1997. *The Southern Forester.*

Balfour, Jr., Robert C. 1975. *This land I have loved.* Tallahassee, FL: Rose Printing Company.

Barrett, DuPre. 1930. A business view of the cut over lands of the south. *Cypress Knee.* 8: 44–46.

Barrow, D. C. 1916. Chancellor of the University of Georgia in "What people think." *Forest Club Annual.* 1:8.

Bates, William M. 1967. James Fowler—Pioneer tree planter. *TOPS.* 2, no. 3:10, 15.

Bennett, Howard. 1990. 50 years of Miss Georgia Forestry. *TOPS.* 24, no. 2:39–40.

Bishop, G. N. and B. F. Grant. 1957. Golden anniversary: Our first fifty years. *Cypress Knee.* 33: 10–15, 104–9.

Blalock, Tommy. 1959. Georgia's summer foresters learn by doing. *Georgia Agriculturalist.* 51, no. 1: 8–10.

Boerker, Richard H. D. 1945. *Behold our green mansions: A book about American forests.* Chapel Hill: University of North Carolina Press.

Brooks, Robert P. 1956. *The University of Georgia under sixteen administrations: 1785–1955.* Athens: University of Georgia Press.

Brown, E. O. 1939. The senior camp log. University of Georgia George Foster Peabody School of Forestry. Duplicated.

Brown, Leon. 1982. W. Kirk Sutlive: GFA past president 1947–1949. *TOPS.* 15, no. 1: 12–13.

_____. 1982. Jim L. Gillis, Jr.: GFA president 1961–1962. *TOPS.* 15, no. 2: 10–11.

_____. 1982. 75 years of GFA—An anniversary special. *TOPS.* 15, no. 2: 26–28.

_____. 1982. Harley Langdale, Jr.: GFA president 1963–1964. *TOPS.* 15, no. 3: 8–9.

Brown, R. Harold. 2002. *The greening of Georgia: The improvement of the environment in the twentieth century.* Macon: Mercer University Press.

Bruncken, Ernest. 1900. *North American forests and forestry: Their relations to the national life of the American people.* New York: G. P. Putnam's Sons.

Burleigh, Thomas D. 1923. The Division of Forestry. *The Forest Club Annual.* 1: 6–9.

Butler, Carroll B. 1998. *Treasures of the longleaf pines naval stores.* Shalimar, FL: Tarkel Publishing.

Cameron, Frank K. 1939. Charles Holmes Herty. *Journal of the American Chemical Society.* 61: 1619–22.

Campbell, W. Andy. 1978. The School of Forest Resources: University of Georgia. University of Georgia School of Forest Resources. Duplicated.

Carlyle, Thomas. [1833] 2002. *Sartor resartus: The life and opinions of Herr Teufelsdrockh.* LexisNexis: Gridiron Edition.

Chapman, H. H. 1935. *Professional forestry schools report: Giving the comparative status of those institutions that offered instruction in professional forestry for the school year 1934–35.* Washington, D.C.: Society of American Foresters.

_____. 1936. Letter to Governor Eugene Talmadge of Georgia. *Journal of Forestry.* 34, no. 4: 431.

_____. 1936. Letter of reply to Governor Eugene Talmadge of Georgia. *Journal of Forestry.* 34, no. 4: 432.

Clark, Anna. 1997. Volunteers set world record on tree–rific Arbor Day. *Macon Telegraph.* February 22, A1.

Clark, Thomas D. 1984. *The greening of the south: The recovery of land and forest.* Lexington: University of Kentucky Press.

Clepper, Henry and Meyer, Arthur B. (eds.). 1960. *American forestry: Six decades of growth.* Washington, D.C.: Society of American Foresters.

_____. 1971. *Professional forestry in the United States.* Baltimore: The Johns Hopkins Press.

Cowdrey, Albert E. 1983. *This land, this south: An environmental history.* Lexington: University of Kentucky Press.

Darby, Sanford. 1967. Fifty years of seedling production in Georgia. *TOPS.* 1, no. 3: 14.

Doherty, C. P. 1926. Our cabin. *Cypress Knee.* 4: 8–10.

Duerr, William A. (ed.). 1973. *Timber! Problems, prospects, policies.* Ames: Iowa State University Press.

Duncan, Jr., John P. 1967. Georgia forestry's changing times 1967–1997. *TOPS.* 2, no. 1: 32, 36.

Dyer, Thomas G. 1985. *The University of Georgia: A bicentennial history, 1785–1985.* Athens: University of Georgia Press.

Earley, Lawrence S. 2004. *Looking for longleaf: The fall and rise of an American forest.* Chapel Hill: University of North Carolina Press.

Eldridge, I. M. 1929. Suwannee forest. *Cypress Knee.* 7: 66–68.

Felty, Jr., Hilra H. 1970. A history of the School of Forest Resources, University of Georgia (1906–1969). Athens: School of Forest Resources Master of Forest Resources Problem.

Fickle, James E. 1980. *The new south and the "new competition": Trade association development in the southern pine industry.* Urbana: University of Illinois Press.

Fitzgerald, Charlie. N.d. Typescript.

Flinchum, D. M. 1971. Criteria for the design of recreation areas on flood plains of the north Georgia piedmont. Master's thesis, University of Georgia.

Forest Club Annual. 1917. 1.

Forest Club of the University of Georgia, The. 1914–1923. Minutes of the Forest Club. School of Forestry, University of Georgia.

Forest History Society. 2005. *Stories of the forest: A campaign to put forest history to work.* Forest History Society pamphlet. Durham, NC.

Garrison, P. M. 1929. Practicing industrial forestry in southern pine. *Cypress Knee.* 7: 63–65.

George Foster Peabody School of Forestry. 1939. Program for the presentation of the bust of George Foster Peabody. April 27. George Foster Peabody School of Forestry. Duplicated.

Georgia Forestry Association. 1933. Articles of association: Georgia Forestry Association by-laws and constitution. Duplicated.

[Georgia Forestry Association]. 1966. *TOPS.* I, no. I.

_____. 1968. Forest industry safety inspections. *TOPS.* 2, no. 3: 4.

_____. 1968. Meet William M. Oettmeier—Longtime G. F. A. member. *TOPS.* 2, no. 4: 10

_____. 1969. Merger creates new forest institute. *TOPS.* 3, no. 3: 20.

_____. 1982. Georgia's national tree farmer of the year. *TOPS.* 15, no. I: 20.

_____. 1982. GFA gives first woods arson awards. *TOPS.* 15, no. I: 26.

Georgia Forestry Commission. 1956. 50 years of progress. *Georgia Forestry.* 9, no. 9: I

_____. 1956. From then…'Til now: History of Peabody Forestry School. *Georgia Forestry.* 9, no. 9: 2, 9.

_____. 1956. Forestry school boasts well-qualified faculty members. *Georgia Forestry.* 9, no. 9: 5–6.

_____. 1956. Students encouraged in campus activities. *Georgia Forestry.* 9, no. 9: 8.

Gerrell, Pete. 1998. *The illustrated history of the naval stores (turpentine) industry with artifact guide, home remedies, recipes and jokes.* Crawfordville, FL: SYP Press.

_____. 1999. *Old trees: The illustrated history of logging virgin timber in the southeastern U.S.* Crawfordville, FL: SYP Press.

Grant, B. F. 1925. Activities of the Forestry Club. *Cypress Knee.* 7: 16.

Graves, Henry S. 1930. Trends in forestry education. *Cypress Knee.* 8: 49–52.

Gunter, John, Dangerfield Jr., Coleman, and Martin, Dennis. 1991. The new property tax and your timber. *TOPS.* 25, no. 4: 6–7, 9.

Hargreaves Jr., L. A. 1953. The Georgia Forestry Commission—objectives, organization, policies and procedures. Ph.D. diss., University of Michigan.

_____ and Campbell, W. A. 1979. School of Forest Resources research for the 1980s. University of Georgia School of Forest Resources. Duplicated.

_____. 1982. Forestry education—Prospects for the future. *TOPS.* 15, no. I: 18–19.

_____. 1990. The red eye rules of administration. University of Georgia School of Forest Resources. Duplicated.

Harman, C. B. 1926. Our forests today and twenty years hence. *Cypress Knee.* 4: II–I2.

Hayler, Nicole (ed.). 2002. *Sound wormy: Memoir of Andrew Gennett, lumberman.* Athens: University of Georgia Press.

Haynes, W. N. 1982. Forest business management at the School of Forest Resources, University of Georgia. *TOPS.* 15, no. 3: 12–13.

_____. 1991. Daniel B. Warnell. *TOPS.* 23, no. 2: 14–15.

Healy, Robert G. 1985. *Competition for land in the American south.* Washington, D.C.: The Conservation Foundation.

Herty, Charles H. 1903. A new method of turpentine orcharding. USDA Bureau of Forestry Bulletin No. 40.

_____. 1929. The future of cellulose. *Cypress Knee.* 7: 60–62.

_____. 1937. The pulp and paper laboratory at Savannah: Its history, operation and future. Savannah Pulp and Paper Laboratory. Duplicated.

Hodgson, Richard S. 1970. *In quiet ways—George H. Mead: The man and the company.* Dayton: The Mead Corporation.

Holbrook, Alfred H. 1958. Peabody gifts. Typescript. 4p.

Hopkins, Jr., Milton N. 2001. *In one place: The natural history of a Georgia farmer.* St. Simons Island, GA: The Saltmarsh Press.

Industrial Department Seaboard Air Line Railroad Company. 1956. Golden anniversary: George Foster Peabody School of Forestry. *Forestry Bulletin.* 46: n.p.

International Paper Company. 1997. *A history of southlands experiment forest.* New York: International Paper Company.

Izlar, Robert L. 1972. The Hebard Lumber Company in the Okefenokee Swamp: Thirty-six years of southern logging history. Master's problem, University of Georgia.

Izlar, Bob. 1984. University of Georgia Center for Forest Business Management. American Pulpwood Association Technical Release 84-R-14, Washington, DC, 2p.

_____. 1989. Statement before the Subcommittee on Conservation and Forestry. In **Hearing before the Subcommittee on Conservation and Forestry of the Committee on Agriculture, Nutrition and Forestry, United States Senate, 101st Cong., 1st sess., On the effects of tax reform on the timber industry, 13 March 1989, Macon, Georgia.** U.S. Government Printing Office, Washington, D.C., 147p., p. 34–39.

_____. 1990. General Assembly sets stage for landmark ad valorem tax reform. *TOPS.* 24, no. 1: 8–10.

_____. 1990. Conservation use amendment will keep Georgia green and growing. *TOPS.* 24, no. 3: 6–7.

_____. 1990. Conservation use amendment passes overwhelmingly. *TOPS.* 24, no. 4: 6–7.

_____. 1991. Conservation use legislation—summary. *TOPS.* 25, no. 1: 14–15

_____. 1991. One year after Amendment Three: Where are we? *TOPS.* 25, no. 4: 6–7, 9.

_____. 1991. Conservation use legislation: Update II. *TOPS.* 25, no. 3: 6.

_____. 1991. Jayhole legend. Jayhole Club, University of Georgia Chapter. Duplicated.

_____. 1995. Farm, forestry and environmental groups agree. *TOPS.* 29, no. 1: 33.

Izlar, Wright. 1990. Interview by author. Waycross, GA. 5 October.

Jayhole Club, University of Georgia Chapter. 1976. Constitution and bylaws. University of Georgia School of Forest Resources. Duplicated.

Karina, Stephen J. 1987. *The University of Georgia College of Agriculture: An administrative history, 1785–1985.* Athens: University of Georgia College of Agriculture.

Kinney, J. P. [1917] 1972. *The development of forest law in America.* Reprint, New York: Arno Press.

Kollock, J. T. 1932. Through the years with the alumni. *Cypress Knee.* 10: 57.

Lancaster, John E. 2002. *Judge Harley and his boys: The Langdale story.* Macon: Mercer University Press.

Langdale, Jr., Harley. 1991. As I remember it. *Forest Farmer.* 50, no. 6: 6–9.

_____. 2005. Interview by author. Valdosta, GA. 7 September.

Leavell, Chuck. 2001. *Forever green: The history and hope of the American Forest.* Atlanta: Longstreet Press.

McCaffrey, J. E. 1967. Georgia forestry's changing times 1907–1937. *TOPS.* 2, no. 1:5, 28–29, 33.

MacCleery, Douglas W. 1992. *American forests: A history of resiliency and recovery.* U.S. Department of Agriculture Forest Services, FS-540.

Marckworth, Gordon D. 1932. A history of the Georgia Forest School. *Cypress Knee.* 10: 54–56, 75–83.

Mathis, Ray (ed.). 1974. *"Uncle Tom" Reed's memoir of the University of Georgia.* Athens: University of Georgia Libraries Miscellanea Publications No. 11.

May, Jack T. 1996. Letter to Dean Arnett C. Mace, Jr. December 12.

McClelland, W. Craig. 1995. *Union Camp Corporation: A legacy of leadership.* The Newcomen Society of the Unites States, Newcomen Publication No. 1453.

McSwiney, E. V. 1967. Georgia forestry's changing times 1937–1967. *TOPS*. 2, no. 1: 15, 21, 24.

Myers, Jr., J. Walter. 1988. *Impact of forestry associations on productivity in the south's forests*. U.S. Department of Agriculture Forest Service, Miscellaneous Publication No. 1458.

_____ 1991. The Walter Myers era, 1951–1982. *Forest Farmer*. 50, no. 6: 12–14.

Nesbit, W. A. 1929. The exclusive club. *Cypress Knee*. 7: 12–14.

Norton, Eliot. 1923. The interest of banks and trust companies in forestry. *Cypress Knee*. 1: 28–31.

Odum, Eugene P. and Turner, Monica G. 1990. The Georgia landscape: A changing resource. In *Changing landscapes: An ecological perspective*. New York: Springer-Verlag.

Oettmeier, W. M. 1933. Forestry in southeast Georgia. *Cypress Knee*. 11: 39–41.

Oettmeier Jr., William M. 1991. Why? *Forest Farmer*. 50, no. 6: 10–11.

Outland III, Robert B. 2004. *Tapping the pines: The naval stores industry in the American south*. Baton Rouge: Louisiana State University Press.

Patterson, Archie E. 1994. Ethics in forestry: Four self-help questions. In *Ethics in forestry*, edited by Lloyd C. Irland. Portland, OR: Timber Press.

Pikl Jr., I. James. 1966. *A history of Georgia forestry*. Athens: University of Georgia Bureau of Business and Economic Research, Research Monograph No. 2.

Plummer, Gayther L. 1975. 18th century forests in Georgia. *Bulletin of the Georgia Academy of Science*. 33: 1–19.

_____. 1976. Mulberries to soybeans: Changing vegetation patterns. *Bulletin of the Georgia Academy of Science*. 34: 182–191.

Reed, Germaine M. 1995. *Crusading for chemistry: The professional career of Charles Holmes Herty*. Athens: University of Georgia Press.

Reed, Gerry. 1982. Saving the naval stores industry: Charles Holmes Herty's cup-and-gutter experiments 1900–1905. *Journal of Forest History*. 26: 168–75.

Reed, Thomas W. 1935. *David Crenshaw Barrow*. Athens: Published Privately.

_____. 1946. "George Foster Peabody School of Forestry." University of Georgia Library Reed Collection typescript. p. 2123–34.

Roosevelt, President [Theodore]. 1905. The forest in the life of a nation. In *Proceedings of the American Forest Congress*. Washington, D.C.: H. M. Suter Publishing Company.

Roper, Daniel M. 1996. Watson Springs Resort. *North Georgia Journal*. 13, no. 1: 8–11.

Rosser, E. J. 1923. The logging engineers take a trip to the swamps. *The Forestry Club Annual*. 1: 9–16.

Rossoll, Harry. 1968. Why symbols? *TOPS*. 2, no. 4: 6

Savannah Morning News. 2005. Obituary of Burley Brown Lufburrow, 9 June.

School of Forestry. 1950. A forest research program for Georgia. University of Georgia School of Forestry. Duplicated.

School of Forest Resources. 1968. News release announcing name change for the school. University of Georgia School of Forest Resources. Duplicated.

_____. 1981. Seventy-five years service. University of Georgia School of Forest Resources. Duplicated.

Shirley, A. Ray. 1967. Georgia's changing land patterns. *TOPS*. 2, no. 1: 42–43.

Sizemore, William R. 1964. A model procedure for estimating fair market value of southern forest lands with special reference to eminent domain proceedings. Ph.D. diss., University of Georgia.

Society of Xi Sigma Pi, The National Forestry Honor Society, The. 2005. *Newsletter*. 36:1

Soule, Andrew M. 1928. Our forest nursery. *Cypress Knee*. 6:9–11.

_____. 1930. A brief history of the Division of Forestry. *Cypress Knee*. 8: 36–38.

Southern Lumberman. 1939. Georgia Forestry School paneled in native woods. January 15.

State Department of Forestry. 1926. *First biennial report of the state Department of Forestry to the governor and General Assembly of the state of Georgia: 1925–1926*. Atlanta.

Stegeman, John F. 1966. *The ghosts of Herty Field: Early days on a southern gridiron*. Athens: University of Georgia Press.

Stewart, Mart A. 2002. *"What nature suffers to groe": Life, labor, and landscape on the Georgia coast, 1680–1920*. Athens: University of Georgia Press.

Stone, Bonnell H. 1923. The Georgia For[e]stry Association. *The Forestry Club Annual*. 1: 23, 28–30.

Stripling, C. M. 1990. Why I'm for the conservation use amendment: Question no. 3. *TOPS*. 24, no. 3: 10–11.

Student Body, The. 1937. Do you know? 4p.

Superior Pine Products Co. v. United States. 201 Ct. Cl. 73 1 U.S.T.C. ¶9348; 31 AFTR 2d 1134 (1973).

Sutton, V. J. 1968. "Twenty years of green." *TOPS*. 3, no. 1: 4, 30.

Talmadge, Eugene. 1936. Letter to H. H. Chapman. *Journal of Forestry*. 34, no. 4: 432.

Talmadge, Herman E. and Winchell, Mark Royden. 1987. *Talmadge—A political legacy, a political life: A memoir*. Atlanta: Peachtree Publishers.

Tankersley, Larry A., Gunter, John E. and Dangerfield, Jr., Coleman W. 1990. House Resolution 836, proposed ad valorem tax changes. *TOPS*. 24, no. 3: 8–9.

Thurmond, Jr., A. K. 1928. Our club. *Cypress Knee*. 6: 7.

———. 1928. Cypress Knees. *Cypress Knee*. 6: 49.

Trowbridge, K. S. 1929. Georgia Forest School shows progress. *Cypress Knee*. 7: 35–38.

Underwood, Rudy and Ray, Bob. 1990. Status of property tax-related legislation. *TOPS*. 24, no. 2: 18–20.

Union Bag-Camp Athletic Association. 1960. In the ground and growing—quite a feat: 100,000,000 trees. *The Digester*. 25, no. 3: 5.

Union Bag Camp Paper Corporation. 1959. Nursery announcement. Typescript.

U.S. Department of Agriculture Agricultural Marketing Service. 1957. *Georgia agricultural facts 1900–1956*. Georgia Agricultural Extension Service Bulletin 511 (revised). Athens.

U.S. Department of Agriculture Forest Service. 1979. History of cooperation between the School of Forest Resources and the U.S. Dept. of Agriculture through the Division of Forest Pathology and the Forest Service. USDA Forest Service. Duplicated.

University of Georgia. 2005. Georgia Room School of Forest Resources vertical file. University of Georgia Ilah Dunlap Little Memorial Library Hargrett Rare Book Special Collections. Duplicated.

Van Den Avyle, M. J. 1983. History of the Georgia Cooperative Fishery Research Unit. Georgia Cooperative Fish and Wildlife Unit. Duplicated.

Walker, Laurence C. 1991. *The southern forest: A chronicle*. Austin: University of Texas Press.

[Warren, B. Jack]. 1991. Forest farmers association through the years. *Forest Farmer*. 50, no. 6: 18–25, 28, 30, 32, 34–36, 38, 47.

Weddell, D. J. 1943. Your School of Forestry. *Cypress Knee*. 21: 13.

———. 1946. The war years at the school. *Cypress Knee*. 22: 17.

Whitehead, T. H. 1976. Georgia's nineteenth century chemists. *Bulletin of the Georgia Academy of Science*. 34: 200–03.

Wiggins, B. Lawton. 1905. The attitude of educational institutions toward forestry. In *Proceedings of the American Forest Congress*. Washington, D.C.: H. M. Suter Publishing Company.

Winn Jr., Courtland S. 1932. Through the years with the alumni. *Cypress Knee*. 10: 58–59.

Wright, Jr., J. B. 1914. *The University of Georgia alma mater*. University of Georgia.

Index

About the Author

Bob Izlar with Georgia Bulldog helmet autographed by Heisman Trophy winner Herschel Walker, 2003. *Courtesy Frank M. Riley, Jr.*

Bob Izlar is a native of Waycross, Georgia—the biggest city in the biggest county in the biggest state east of the Mississippi River. Unlike many of the people he knows and describes in this volume, he is not from a forestry family, although both sides of his family have owned timberland for many generations. He grew up camping, fishing, trapping, hunting, and roaming the woods along the Satilla River swamps and exploring his beloved Okefenokee Swamp.

After barely graduating from Waycross High in 1967 and rejecting a full scholarship to read forestry at the University of the South, he matriculated at the University of Georgia, where he paid his way running a survey crew, delivering parcel post, washing dishes, and raising flies. He did somewhat better in Athens and proudly became a "Double Dawg" with bachelor's and master's degrees in forest resources in 1971 and 1972, along with a commission as "an officer and gentleman" in

the Army of the United States. Realizing he knew not one blessed thing about business, he earned an MBA from Georgia Southern University in 1977 while working full time.

After two years active military service, mostly working with dogs in Asia, he began his checkered forestry career, which took him from Georgia to Mississippi and back again. In that time, he hustled pulpwood; drove a raggedy big stick log truck with no brakes, coolant, or transmission; worked a territory from the eastern shore of Maryland to Arizona; saw every pulpmill in the South; became a lobbyist with no formal training (and it certainly showed); traveled in foreign lands; ran two state forestry associations, and landed back at his alma mater in Georgia's northland as director of the Warnell School of Forestry and Natural Resources' Center for Forest Business, where he is dreading retirement in 2021.

For the last thirty years or so, he has actually had two paying jobs at the same time. Somehow, the secretary of the Army put up with his lack of a proper haircut and untrimmed mustache long enough for him to be promoted (who knows how) to full colonel in the United States Army Reserve. At one time, the Army said he was a good shot if sufficiently motivated.

For those who know him best, he is the "poster boy" for the late Senator Herman Talmadge's adage that "hard work and perseverance will overcome an incredible amount of stupidity." In his plentiful spare time, he still loves to talk about the "Okfinoke" to the few who will still listen. The swamp, family, and friends have been his inspiration and retreat.

He counts the highlight of his lobbying phase as the time he had his picture made with UGA V. There is still heated debate on the third floor of the Capitol about which Dawg was the ugliest.

Most days you can find him within the cloistered walls of academe, but not if there is barbeque to be had, especially if he does not have to pay.

He says he has been so awe-inspired with the delightful task of writing this slim but highly scholarly and elegant tome that his next book, forthcoming soon, will be the highly anticipated *An Anthology of Minor Scottish Poets of the Early 1740s*.

Cognitate illos canes! [1]

Loading a gum wagon, ca. early 1900s. *Courtesy Ted Walker/USFS*